Americans Speak

"One Thing
I Would Do For
Our Country Is..."

Susan Abel Lieberman

With 65 Voters,
48 High School Students.
and an Explanation of the Federal Budget

ISBN-13:
978-1535144186

ISBN-10:
1535144181

Ordering Information:
Amazon.com
Susan A. Lieberman, Ph.D.
susan@lieberman.net
713 443 7250

TABLE OF CONTENTS

I. INTRODUCTION

What is it we Americans want for our country? Beyond the media headlines and the polls that frame for us what we will be discussing, what do we really hope for our communities, our families and ourselves? In this moment when there is so much dissension and disagreement among us, when our leaders seem more caught up in resistance and reaction, when an election season of unexpected outcomes has astounded us, isn't it just the right time to talk ideas?

All this was brought home for me one evening in March. My husband and I were invited to join eight others at a book club dinner party. Book talked morphed to politics, and in the course of that evening, nearly everyone commented on "…one thing I would do…"

This talk about what people wanted to do seemed so much richer than which party was more at fault for gridlock or which candidate was more reprehensible. "I wish I could hear this from a hundred people," I told my husband driving home. The next morning, I woke up knowing that was exactly what I wanted to do, to get a hundred men and women of all ages, races and backgrounds to answer the question: IF I WERE IN CHARGE, ONE THING I WOULD DO FOR OUR COUNTRY IS…?

This collection of replies to that question is an effort to hear (without filters) what we the people think is important for the country. It's so easy to substitute drama for substance. We complain that our leaders lack vision, but it isn't only our leaders who are struggling. It has been surprisingly difficult to find people willing to speak up. In response to perhaps a thousand emails to family, friends, friends of friends and complete strangers, only sixty-five people across the country responded to the IF I WERE IN CHARGE challenge. These voices are increased by dozens of San Diego high school students whose wishes are in the Voices of the Next Generation section.

A huge THANK YOU to all of you who participated. A thousand thank yous. That standard line, "It wouldn't have happened without you" is, in this instance, completely literal. You all are an exclusive, classy group who are not afraid to think about important issues, take a stance, and put your name and photograph on it. Although you are few in number, my hunch is that each of you represents thousands more silent citizens

You worried about making good choices. You were often troubled that you didn't know enough about the issue you cared about and might not sound "smart enough." You understood that speaking out was not going to fix America and that implementation strategies were complex. And yet, you were not afraid to stand up and say, "I care about this."

Not a single one of you is, as far as I know, currying voter favor or looking for favorable press. No one is getting a donation for representing a position. You spoke from head and heart, for yourselves and for children and grandchildren. It is a privilege to be able to present your thoughts.

II. LESSONS LEARNED

We Find It Difficult to Talk About Policy

It is easier, much easier, to get people to talk about the peculiarities and personalities of people in politics. Is Ted Cruz really Lucifer? Does Hilary deceive us? Is Donald Trump on an ego trip? Will we ever hear from Marco Rubio again? Even the busiest people find time for this chatter. But focusing on policy questions is so much harder. If we leave the generalities behind and dive deep into any issue, we are perplexed by the complexity of differing points of view, overwhelmed by information and disappointed there is little clarity around a strategy for solving the problem.

Since there in little consensus among the Replies from voters, you might wonder what to make of all this. Make of it what you will. What I make of it is that there is a deep yearning in all of us to be better, get better, do better. Figuring out what better means and how to get there feels overwhelming. So mostly we begin with issues we know most about from our lives. There is a strong desire for greater civility. Education and climate change are popular themes. So too are voting and finances, but no one honed in on foreign policy or terrorism. While abortion rights and a conservative Supreme Court Justice are included, there is no reply spotlighting the Congressional budgeting process or care of veterans, but you'll see replies about immigration and the elderly. I thought surely some people would address homelessness or tax fraud or privacy, but it didn't happen in this sample. Certainly other voters, had they been reached and chosen to respond, would have broadened the already diverse list. The student responses both amplify and add to the adult replies. This small sample does open a window on what comes to mind when thoughtful, intelligent men and women are pressed to talk about policy without any special influence, and it underscores the enormous challenge of devising strategies to address our problems and opportunities.

Just in these few months of work, I have become more convinced – and I was pretty convinced when I started – that we have to find ways to talk with one another, respect each other's concerns, and find compromises that serve the greater good as best we can. Several Replies address just this. The perfect IS the enemy of the good. Many ideas in this book do not align with my political views, but they represent large segments of the population who silently agree with a given position and deserve to be heard civilly. We all deserve to be heard civilly, but that requires we also hear other's civilly.

In the heat of a political conversation, an acquaintance once told me that her side had simply compromised way too much and there was no room in the political system for any further compromise. Her words made me feel physically ill. I had to leave the gathering and go quiver in my car. If we refuse the notion of compromise, we are rejecting a belief in the democratic process. In a democracy, we start with a vision. And then we see what is possible factoring in the visions of others.

You will read some of these ideas and, perhaps, think, "Well, that's a good idea, but it's impossible to implement." Nelson Mandela, for 27 years a political prisoner, ultimately brokered the end of apartheid and became President of South Africa. He counseled, "It always seems impossible until it's done." It is easy to see how things are impossible. But it is liberating to make a space in our conversation for the impossible as a beginning point in imagining a way forward.

Ideas are content. They need a context in which to bloom. Our culture provides that evolving context. We are not good at predicting when the conditions are right for an idea to explode, but if we encourage the articulation of lots and lots of ideas, some of them will take root.

Why People Chose Not to Reply

It was far more challenging to elicit responses than I imagined when I impetuously decided to start this project and publish the results in five months. Most of the people contacted passed on the opportunity. Their reasons, when given, were as interesting as the Replies.

Too hard: "I started and then I found I didn't know enough about the issue I selected, so I started to do some research and realized it was way more complicated than I realized." Versions of that experience came back to me more than once. The realities of designing change intimidate lots of us. We want to be thoughtful when we speak, and we are often overwhelmed by complexity.

Too impractical: Similarly, some people knew what they wanted but were befuddled by how to get there and were uncomfortable articulating an issue they thought didn't have any chance of being successful. Their sense of facing rock solid obstacles had a deadening effect. It felt fruitless to bother talking about a seemingly hopeless idea.

Too many: Lots of people found it too hard to "pick just one". "Wouldn't this be a better question if you asked me for my top five?" a politically engaged lawyer asked. Of course, it's understandable to have more than one issue you'd like to address, and as you will see, some people couldn't resist and slipped in more than one.

Too distracted: Way more than once, I had people tell me, "I just can't think about it right now." We do need some serious stretches of quiet time to think about a response and formulate our thoughts, and life is, for most Americans, busy. There was a paucity of Replies from people with small children and busy jobs. And maybe asking people to think about policy in the middle of tax season was ill-timed. But shouldn't a presidential election season be the time for mulling over policy and reflecting on our most important priorities?

Too public: A retired corporate executive, a wise and thoughtful man, wrote me: "I have reviewed your invitation and will pass. Why? It strikes me as being a little too invasive as well as having a daunting list of issues." A woman in my walking group explained: "I'm kind of private about politics. I don't really want my name and picture out there." She captured the feeling of many. The regulator who worried about her security clearance, the judge who felt it inappropriate to take a public stand, the politician who thought this wasn't the right format – I get it. But, in general, this seemingly prevalent desire for privacy puzzled me.

Everyone isn't into bumper stickers and yard signs or being blatant about party politics at work. But what does it tell us when people don't want to let others know what they think the nation's priorities should be? Do we fear the reactions of friends or colleagues? In this age of expansive social media, are there real dangers in having stated policy positions? Is a penchant for environmental issues or universal health care or infrastructure investment something we ought to keep secret?

Too presumptuous: I reached out to a libertarian acquaintance who had been a successful television journalist and now works on media development aimed at promoting conservative social change with a free enterprise orientation. Her response to the "If I Were In Charge" question was this:

> *I actually think that the biggest problem we face as a country, on both the right and the left, is that the parties are largely populated by arrogant people who believe that if their ideas were followed then they would be able to "fix" us. I'm afraid I have deep issues with the very premise of your question.*

I was surprised by this response because I find most people are well aware of the complexities of managing change and understand that an idea is just that—an idea that has to be addressed in much more complex way if it is to be implemented. I hadn't imagined that anyone would find it arrogant to float an idea we think might make the country better, although I am sure this woman must not be alone in her in her reluctance to have policies applied generally rather than allowing each of us to do what we think is best for us.

There is probably no idea in this book that could be dropped into our government as presented and be well-received by all of us. Every idea must contend with competing ideas, other ways of seeing the world, other wishes for what's most important. That said, let's talk about our ideas anyway. Let's find out why ideas that seem to us so logical are, in fact, not as feasible to implement as expected and why. In the process, we will learn and others will too, and our ideas will evolve. This is how meaningful legislation is produced.

Some groups have access to revenue streams that allow them to support large lobbying and public relations operations to advocate for policies of importance to them. Without resources, it is difficult to compete with these well-funded voices. Here are voices hard to hear in the din.

III. REPLIES

MANDATORY NATIONAL SERVICE AFTER HIGH SCHOOL

> *"It would create an opportunity for young people to connect with others in service to a higher goal, learning how to operate like a team and make compromises on behalf of the common good."*

If I were in charge, one thing I would do for the country is to implement a mandatory year of service for young people following high school graduation. At a time in which technology and other factors have caused individuals to become increasingly self-centered and (ironically) disconnected from the world around them, the intent behind a year of service would be threefold. It would create an opportunity for young people to connect with others in service to a higher goal, learning how to operate like a team and make compromises on behalf of the common good. It would allow them to give back to their community in a meaningful way, build confidence in the power of people, and take pride in impacting the world for the better. And, finally, a mandatory year of service would enable young people to gain deeper perspective and clarity on themselves and the world before pursuing their graduate ambitions - all the more critical in an increasingly complex world.

The hope would be for a program like this to inspire a more connected, empathetic and engaged youth who devote their careers to helping their communities become cleaner, healthier, more resilient and more caring places to live.

━━◆◆◆━━

ABIGALE (ABBY) ABEL

12

is the Global Director of GE Ecomagination, a cross-GE strategic platform for delivering improved economic and environmental returns to customers. Prior to her current role, Abby served as the Strategic Marketing Leader for GE's Renewable Energy business, responsible for leading a global team in providing the industry analysis to support the business' strategic decision-making.

Abby began her career with GE in 2007 as a member of the Experienced Commercial Leadership Program. During her time on program, Abby worked in various roles across GE's Corporate, Energy Financial Services and Energy Strategic Marketing organizations. Abby joined the GE Ecomagination team in 2016.

Abby holds an M.B.A. and Master of Public Policy (M.P.P.) from the University of Michigan as well as a B.A. from Middlebury College.

INFUSE THE SPIRIT OF COMPROMISE AND RESPECT

"I would want to wave a magic wand and instill patience, tolerance, and understanding in every heart."

If I were in charge of the country I would want to infuse the spirit of compromise and respect for others' viewpoints in our elected officials and in the voting public.

And I have not the foggiest idea of how I would go about doing that.

We have reached a terrible point in our history where if you don't agree with me you are my enemy, where compromise—the very practice that made our Constitution possible—is an evil word, and where having experience in governing is not an asset but a liability. Governance is the only profession in which the public wants inexperience rather than experience. Indeed, in this supposed model of democracy, we don't even bother to vote. Do you know that in the primary only 7% of Democrats voted in Texas and only 14% of Republicans voted—at least that is the figure I heard.

Although everyone wants simple answers to complex issues, there are none. If I were in charge, I would want to wave a magic wand and instill patience, tolerance, and understanding in every heart. But the reality is that there aren't any magic wands! Only human beings who are currently frightened of a changing world, worried about the economics of their future, rightly scared of extremism and uncomfortable with those who are "different."

—⊜◆⊜—

MADELEINE G. APPEL

spent 34 years in Houston City Government, the last four of which she was deputy chief of staff to former Mayor Annise D. Parker. After graduation from Smith College, she was a reporter for The Corpus Christi Caller-Times, The Houston Chronicle, and The Insider's Newsletter, a publication of Cowles Communications in New York City. She has served on the boards of and as president of the League of Women Voters of Greater Houston (and the state and national League boards), Houston Achievement Place (HAP), Houston Congregation for Reform Judaism, Jewish Family Service and Scenic America (and the board of Scenic Houston). She is married to Dr. Michael F. Appel. They have two sons and daughters-in-law, Dr. Louis Appel and Jennifer Binford and Dr. Noah Appel and Gila Rosenstock Appel, and five grandchildren, Benjamin and Sarah and Daniela, Ari and Gabriela.

RETURN THE U.S. TO A CONSTITUTIONAL REPUBLIC

"I'd fight to abolish the IRS, the Department of Education, the Department of Energy, the Department of Commerce, and the Department of Housing and Urban Development."

If I were president I'd do all in my power to return the USA to the constitutional republic established by the founders, the constitution that's changed the world for good as has no other document or event in human history. I'd start by appointing a constitutional and Bill of Rights conservative to the Supreme Court.

I'd craft transparency in government legislation that would enable any citizen with a smart phone to easily learn, without media spin, anything and everything about the federal government, about federal laws and regulations, current and under consideration, and about every employee, elected and/or appointed, of the federal government, including contact information and all measure of compensation and benefits. I'd require all agencies of the federal government to respond timely to questions and requests from citizens (as has been the case for the military for many years).

I'd fight to abolish the IRS, the Department of Education, the Department of Energy, the Department of Commerce, and the Department of Housing and Urban Development. To do this I'd press Congress relentlessly, and appoint heads of these agencies whose central charge would be to lead the effort to wind them down and determine whether any of their programs need to be preserved elsewhere because they fall within the purview of the federal government.

I'd craft legislation requiring that every employee of the federal government, elected and/or appointed, be subject to the same federal laws as the rest of the citizens, and vice versa. I'd challenge Congress to apply similar legislation to the Affordable Care Act.

I'd take steps within the constitution to undo the Iran Nuclear Deal and stop the flow of funds to Iran.

I'd enforce existing law relative to our southern border, i.e. build a wall/fence, and keep our border patrol deployed at the border.

AL BAXTER
is a retired multi-discipline engineer, project/program manager, and commissioning authority. Widely recognized successes in public and private sector, industrial plant, infrastructure, process, utilities, healthcare, institutional, and commercial, capital, operational cost reduction, reliability improvement, and organizational development projects and programs. Ten years part owner/ operator of a multi-million dollar design build mechanical contractor operation.

Civic / community service leadership roles as a MUD Director (publicly elected, 12 years, president six years), The Woodlands Joint Powers Agency Trustee (six years, president two years), and South Montgomery County (The Woodlands) YMCA Board of Governors (six years, president two years, and Volunteer of the Year). Past Sustaining President of Houston Junior Forum, Founding member of Bluebonnet Society / Bluebonnet Ball in Bellville, Texas, Member of Second Baptist Church

MAKE EDUCATION MORE AFFORDABLE

> *"The income gap has and will continue to widen."*

If I were in charge I would make education more diverse and affordable. The escalating cost for college is totally out of the affordability range for most low-income families. Real change begins at the top and trickles down. The income gap has and will continue to widen. Making college a priority from early child hood forward is the foundation to success.

Most low-income families see college drifting further away, not because of lack of interest but affordability. To compete in this fast paced international cyberworld involves access as early as possible. Scholarships are offered to the brightest of students, but what about the mid-range student who does not have access to the hardware and software or the proper learning environment to succeed. If our young people are going to continue to lead this country forward, it should be this country's priority to supply them with as many chances and opportunities as we can for success. If I were in charge, my priority would be to implement free education to all who so desire.

BENNY BILLINGS

Born in El Dorado Arkansas, grew up in Milwaukee Wisconsin from age 5 until moving to Houston Texas at age 22. Married at age 35. I have a BS in Communications and Telecommunication and a minor in Radio and Math from Texas Southern University.

I am 55 years of age, I am employed and have witnessed every social economic demographic group at the luxury hotel I've worked at since 1993. I have mentored young, at risk African-American males at Kashmere High School in Houston, Texas. I have seen what happens to boys and girls who don't have father figures at home; they are from low income families where college is not a option because of the cost and more precisely, no one has attended college in past generations, so the expectations don't change. That mindset is super difficult to overcome. Getting a disadvantaged youth to believe in himself is a formidable task considering the crime, drugs, pregnancies and overall hardships surrounding the community. But if we can reach one student, our efforts are not in vain.

OVERHAUL THE EDUCATION SYSTEM

> *"All students learn critical thinking skills."*

If I had the power, I would enlist entertainers, sports figures, the media, retired teachers, community leaders and others to educate the public as to what is appropriate for children developmentally. The goal would be to create activists for overhauling our educational system.

This system is based on sound research. School begins at age four, with a sliding scale tuition-based option for three year olds. Children below the poverty line attend for free. Curriculum for three, four, and five year olds is based on developmentally appropriate play and experience-based learning, including development of gross and fine motor skills, creativity, language skills, self-reliance, collaboration, and a spirit of inquiry.

When a child is ready for first grade (with readiness determined by teachers and parents together), reading and math instruction begins. In grades one - three children learn to read and do basic arithmetic. Experienced-based learning expands children's knowledge of social studies, science, language and creativity. Twice a day outdoor playtime is required. Testing determines a child's readiness to move on to fourth grade with parent and teacher evaluations also given weight. Schools are not allowed to spend time "prepping" for the test. From grade four on, the curriculum includes math, science, history, civics, computer literacy, art, and music. Critical thinking is covered in all areas.

High school students are helped to look realistically at their interests and talents and learn about all kinds of careers. In the junior year, students choose between a college prep curriculum, an extended-year curriculum that gives them an Associate's Degree with readiness to transfer as a junior to a four-year college, or an extended year that grants an associate's degree with certification in a skill. All students learn critical thinking skills.

Many children come to school unable to learn because of crisis in the home. Counseling services that can direct a family to resources to assist should be available to all schools. Similarly, parental education for at-risk children should be available.

PAT BISSONNET

After college, Pat taught English and French then earned a degree
in Developmental Reading and taught reading to middle schoolers and
adults. After years of teaching, she became a training specialist for U. T.
M.D. Anderson. At the age of 42 she went to law school, later becoming
Director of Diversity and Fair Employment Practices for Continental
Airlines. She is currently retired and volunteers in the
public schools. She is married and has two
adult children and two grandchildren.

HEALTH SYSTEM UPGRADES

> *"No one should have extreme financial stress during extreme health stress."*

My major issue is health care. There are many good things about our healthcare system in the U.S., but there are also highly frustrating and ruinous aspects. So, what would I do if I were in charge?

1) Continue on the path of Obama Care, trying to make sure we are ALL in one insurance pool so that we help cover one another. No one should have extreme financial stress during extreme health stress. That is cruel and preventable. A major cause of personal bankruptcy is severe illness, which brings with it catastrophic bills. But I would ensure patients have some "skin in the game" through co-pays and co-insurance. Patients need to care about the cost of their care.

2) We need to make the costs transparent! Just two months ago, I was trying to find out how much normal blood work would be. Neither my provider nor my insurer could give me a procedure code. How could that possibly be?? I got so frustrated that I never did the testing. Won't patients "think twice" if they know that the MRI for their lower back is going to cost $1200, especially if they re told it won't really alter their treatment?

3) I'm in business, and in the business world we obsessively create comprehensive reports that have ALL the information that is pertinent to making complicated decisions. In medicine, we need to make sure, upon leaving the office, that patients receive a written report which describes in plain English the complaint as the doctor understood it, the diagnosis, the proposed treatment, symptoms to watch for, the procedure codes, and the costs. Even auto shops do this. It doesn't have to be time-consuming for the doctor's office, because much of the report would be standard (e.g. Everyone with Type 2 Diabetes would need the same information on diet, etc.) Most of the time, after my parents leave the doctor's office, they can't remember the name of what they have,

they can't pronounce the drug they have been prescribed, they can't remember their doctor's name, or they are unclear as to why a test was ordered. My new provider, UCSD issues an excellent report. Well done UCSD!

4) Teach students from a young age, as part of the school curriculum, more than just basic health topics. Expand the school curriculum to the latest clinical studies results, symptoms of common diseases, and symptoms and treatments for mental illnesses. Everyone needs to know how to track and manage their own medical records.

5) Create national best practices for treating diseases.

LINDA BOLD
A native of Minnesota, spent 23 years mostly in the NYC area in Corporate America in International finance, Business Analysis, M&A, Brand Management, and New Product Development for Kraft, Novartis, Gerber Baby, Clairol/Bristol-Myers Squibb, and Unisys. She was a consultant for start-ups Algaeon (which she named) and MyCell Technologies, and also did extensive consulting for Post Foods, and the Glacier National Park Conservancy. She has an MBA from Indiana University, a BA in Mathematics and Economics from St. Olaf College, and an MA in Psychology from Northcentral University. She was a Board Member for Suited For Success, a NYC organization which helped lower socioeconomic women with job skills and resources. She was also the Co-Founder and Co-Chair of The Gallery at the Public Library in Glen Rock, NJ, providing a place for local artists to display their work.
She now resides in La Jolla, CA.

UNDERSTAND HOW CHILDREN LEARN

"It's been proven that the earlier a talent is recognized the more successful the person will be if their energy is channeled in that direction."

A cross the board, young Americans fared poorly compared to those in the other countries studied. They tied for last, with Italy and Spain, in math skills. In problem solving, they again performed at the bottom of the pack, with Ireland, Poland, and the Slovak Republic. U.S. millennials also had lower literacy scores than peers in 15 out of 22 countries, tied with a few, and outperformed only peers in Italy and Spain. Younger members of the cohort, who presumably grew up under the last decade of high-stakes accountability initiatives, were no more competitive globally than older millennials. (Education Week, 5/15/16)

The United States ranks seventeenth out of forty countries ranked in overall educational performance. If I could change one thing in this country it would be addressing these deficits. It would be mandatory that each child be tested to see HOW they learn.

In elementary school: Are they visual, auditory, hands on? I don't believe that everyone learns in the same way. Just like there is cognitive IQ, there is social IQ, Emotional IQ and so forth. I think identifying learning patterns early on and developing others like social skills will help a child be a success for the rest of his or her life.

In middle school, the most rebellious age group, do they have talents that are apparent? It's been proven that the earlier a talent is recognized the more successful the person will be if their energy is channeled in that direction.

In high school: If college is not on the horizon, is there vocational training the student can receive? These options are not available in every school. A child may graduate but have no options until they learn a trade in prison. We need to care more about each graduate.

It will take resources and a revolutionary way of thinking to implement a program like this, but it will build a better nation and hopefully better presidential candidates.

SHARON BRIER
is the founder of The Children's Museum of Houston.
She has been a real estate agent since 1980 and is a
volunteer for many non-profit organizations.

DEPARTMENT OF PEACE

> *"We badly need a new way of looking at things."*

If I were in charge, one thing I would do for this country is create a Peace Department with a Cabinet level Peace Secretary. This idea isn't new to me. Dennis Kucinich has proposed it as law every year since 2001, including during his 2004 and 2008 Presidential runs. And it was proposed in 1793 by Benjamin Rush, a Founding Father and signer of the Declaration of Independence.

We have a Defense Department, which has always functioned more as its original name: War Department. All presidents take seriously their role of Commander-in-Chief and listen to the advice of the Secretaries of the Army, Navy, Air Force, Marines and their generals and admirals, etc.

We badly need a new way of looking at things. I would love to replace the War/Defense Department with the Peace Department but concede that is very unrealistic for generations to come. (However, if same-sex marriage could happen in my lifetime, why not this in the lifetime of my grandchildren?)

The Peace Secretary and Department would be tasked with discovering areas of cooperation instead of hostility, both domestically and internationally. They would have to cooperate with, and ideally would control, affairs of state and trade, since these are traditionally major sources of conflict.

Not only heads of state and captains of industry would be consulted. The world would be scoured for innovative ideas, be they found in small groups, local communities, large countries or entire regions. Solutions would be promulgated globally to create a world in which all could live peacefully on Mother Earth.

SUSAN KENT CAKARS
Editor of psychology, children's,
and educational books and
longtime peace activist.

FREE EARLY CHILDHOOD EDUCATION

> *"What if we think
> of early childhood education not
> so much as an expense but an
> investment that down the line
> yields a significant
> return?"*

Education is my platform because I believe that if we solve for education, we solve for so many other ills that take our time and our resources.

Doing a better job of education for young people means we can do a better job with employment, with reducing early incarceration, with physical health and mental health. Education allows people to know about the dangers of obesity, high cholesterol and high blood pressure. An education facilitates participation in mainstream society and that seems likely to reduce depression and abuse. It would, I believe, help us with global competitiveness and not put us at risk for jeopardizing our standing in the world.

I would have children be able to start free public school at 2 1/2 with a full day option. Imagine how that would help mothers be able to go to work to support their families or to go to school free of the heavy expense of day care.

Yes, there is a cost. But what if we think of early childhood education not so much as an expense but an investment that down the line yields a significant return? This is what research done by all sorts of investigators from neuroscientists to economists are showing us. How much would we need to reduce incarceration expenses to make this pay off? What would the health care savings be? What if immigrant children who came here as little kids arrived in first grade knowing how to speak English?

If we value the future of our nation, mustn't we value our children?

ELIZABETH CAMPBELL
is a frequent speaker, training facilitator and writer
on the topic of diversity and inclusion and related
employment law issues, Campbell is partner and the
chief diversity officer at the law firm of Andrews Kurth.
She received her J.D. degree from the University of Michigan and
her B.A. from American University.
She is the mother of two sons.

STOP FOOD INSUFFICIENCY

> *"A healthy child is more likely to age well and take a more active part in life."*

If I were in charge of the country, one thing I'd do is ensure that no American child or family for that matter went to bed hungry.

The United States Department of Agriculture in 2014 estimated 15.3 million children under 18 lived in households "where they are unable to consistently access enough nutritious food necessary for a healthy life". In 2015 the number was closer to 16 million or 1 out of 5 children. Food insecurity is not just an urban problem but exists in suburbs and rural areas as well.

Good nutrition – particularly beginning in the earliest years of childhood – affects current and future physical and mental health. Providing a more positive start in life enhances performance in school, relationships, future careers and life choices. A healthy child is more likely to age well and take a more active part in life. Ensuring food secure households in America will also guarantee that no parent will have to go hungry themselves to provide food for their child.

Surely in a country such as ours this is not a dream but a real possibility.

PATRICIA MARSH CAVANAUGH
is a native mid-Westerner who is retired from
higher education administration and lives happily with her
husband in Houston, Texas where winters are milder
and she can garden throughout the year.

BALANCE THE BUDGET

> *"Does it make sense to spend half as much on education as we do on interest?"*

If I were in charge the one thing I would do for the country is put us on sound financial footing. At current interest rates, interest on debt is 6%, but interest rates are at a historic low. As they return to normal, interest on debt will eat a larger portion of our budget. Where will this money come from?

Of more concern are the entitlement programs. Today Medicare and social security consume 50% of the national budget. (See federal spending charts in Chapter VII).

In 1940, the life expectancy of a 65-year-old was almost 14 additional years; today it is almost 21 years. By 2035, the number of older Americans will increase from 48 million today to 79 million. There are currently 2.8 workers for each Social Security beneficiary. By 2035, there will be 2.1 workers for each beneficiary. How will fewer workers bear the burden of 60% more beneficiaries? Does it make sense to spend half as much on education as we do on interest?

The solutions are ugly. There is no question that the entitlement programs are important and necessary, but I believe it is time to face the hard truths. Reign them in. Suffer. Don't give it back to the rich in tax breaks. Balance the budget. Six percent more to education would make a huge difference.

Raise the age for social security and Medicare to 70. Will it be a hardship? Yes! But we are spending our children's future.

Long term, the country and its people will be far better off if we do what is right today.

SUSAN CEJKA

Prior to joining Grant Cooper & Associates, Sue Cejka founded
and later sold St. Louis-based Cejka & Company, a healthcare
consulting and search firm. Started in 1981 as a one-woman operation,
the firm grew to a professional staff of more than 100. At the time it was
acquired, it ranked as the 2nd largest healthcare executive search firm
in the country. Ms. Cejka was a recipient of the Ernst & Young/Merrill
Lynch/INC Magazine Entrepreneur of the Year Award.
She spent her early career as a CPA.

LGBTQ EQUALITY

> *"I can't imagine losing my home or my job, or being asked to leave a restaurant simply for being myself and for loving another human being."*

If I were in charge, one thing I would do for this country is enact Lesbian, Gay, Bisexual, Transgender, and Queer (LGBTQ) equality legislation. I have friends and family within the LGBTQ community, and I've heard about the kind of discrimination they face on a daily basis. I can't imagine losing my home or my job, or being asked to leave a restaurant simply for being myself and for loving another human being. Nor can I imagine being unable to create a family with my partner due to adoption discrimination. This is in addition to the daily fear of bullying, violence, and sometimes, death.

If I were in charge, I would enact non-discrimination legislation so that people wouldn't be discriminated against simply because of their sexual identity or orientation. I understand that this is a religious issue for many people, but I believe in a firm separation of church and state. In addition, the science is showing more and more that sexual identity and orientation is not a choice – it is imbedded in a person's DNA. This is the 21st century – no one should have to face these kinds of fears simply for being who they were born to be. We're better than this America – let's show the world how great we can be.

⎯⎯➣⬧⬤⬧⬢⎯⎯

ANGELLE CONANT

is an artist, musician, writer and geek living in the
great state of Texas with her techy husband, babbling baby girl,
and two wise cats. She loves Doctor Who, DIY projects, and chocolate.
Lots and lots of chocolate. To hear about her latest projects
follow her blog, our.lonestar.life, or follow her
on Twitter @angelleconant.

FOCUS ON RENEWABLE ENERGY

> *"Climate change affects everyone— rich and poor, smart and foolish, all races, nationalities, and classes of people."*

If I could change one thing, it would be to give primary attention to the environment, particularly in regard to energy and climate change.

After a recent major flood in the Houston area, the Houston Chronicle noted that Texas climate overall is getting hotter and drier, but with frequent floods and other weather disasters. This is a problem much larger than Texas. In a recent episode on Vice TV, Shane Smith points out that energy is the biggest problem we face today—how we use it and how we get it. We have to phase out fossil fuels whose carbon emissions result in melting ice, rising oceans, and earth's land sinking.

We need to develop and use more renewable energy, create proper grid storage, and develop nuclear power through fusion. The advantage of the latter is that it requires no energy going in to produce energy. All this has implications for our whole earth, and in the worst scenario, most of us may not survive resulting disasters. So, not much else would matter if we're not alive.

Climate change affects everyone—rich and poor, smart and foolish, all races, nationalities, and classes of people. Literally everyone. That is why it's tops on my list.

DONNA R. COPELAND
has a Ph.D. in clinical psychology and practiced
in Houston for 25 years. She is now film critic and
feature writer for Texas Art & Film,
www.texasartfilm.com,
and has a blog,
Dr. Donna's Film Reviews,
http://drdonnasfilmreviews.blogspot.com/?m=0

NATIONALIZE MEDICAL EQUIPMENT

> *"I believe that we can knock a big hole in the patients' costs with one particular initiative."*

I don't want to take over the healthcare industry, nor do I want the government to destroy its innovation and entrepreneurship, but I believe that we can knock a big hole in the patients' costs with one particular initiative: nationalize the nation's medical equipment and make the United States Government the single medical equipment purchaser in the future. Then, I would prohibit all medical services vendors from charging for use of medical equipment since they would no longer be the owners of the equipment. The American people would be the owners of all medical equipment. Here's how it would work:

Any medical services entity that is depreciating medical equipment against their tax liability would submit a complete list of the equipment to the IRS along with the net book value remaining on the equipment. The IRS would pay them for the net book value of all of their equipment and take ownership of the equipment. All medical entities would submit capital expenditure requests along with the justification to an oversight committee for approval. If approved, the government purchases the equipment from the manufacturer and delivers it to the medical services entity. From that point forward, medical services entities would be allowed to charge only for people costs and operating costs, but no charges for medical equipment. Operating costs would include salaries, facility costs, utilities, supplies, etc.

The cost of nationalizing all our medical equipment would come from a surcharge on the income taxes of the top 50% of taxpayers equal to 10% of their tax liability calculated in the normal manner. Eg. If your tax liability is $100,000, then the surcharge is $10,000. This surcharge continues until the bill for the medical equipment is paid. (2014 Tax Revenues were $1.7 Trillion. The surcharge would be $170 Billion.) Annual revenues for the medical equipment industry are about $90 Billion. If the equipment is depreciated over 10 years, there would be about $450 Billion of net book value. Less than three years of surcharges. After the initial bill is paid, the medical equipment budget of the U.S. government would become part of the annual U.S. budget and paid for by tax revenues.

While this plan does tax the upper income group, it is not regressive. Those in the lower 50% of tax payers or the 50% of the population that pays no taxes would not face a surcharge. The government would use its purchasing power to bargain for the best prices for medical equipment, subject to usual government kickbacks, and political deals. Of course, all kinds of financial implications need to be worked out, but this is a start.

DAVID DANIEL
is a Harvard educated man who spent four decades in the oil service industry. Recently retired from his position as Division President of National Oilwell Varco, Inc., he spends a substantial amount of time observing our dysfunctional government's attempt to operate in the effective and efficient manner that we demand of our public companies. He is married with one daughter and four grandsons.

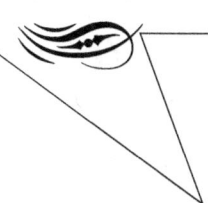

IMPROVEMENTS IN HOW WE VOTE

> *"Encourage our voting populace to vote each and every time there is an election."*

If I were in charge, one thing I'd do for the country is focus on voting reform and voter engagement. While I'm no expert on the topic, I know my own voting history and how it must reflect others' experiences.

When I became eligible to vote (18 years of age, in the United States) I was intimidated by the process. I felt that an uneducated vote would be more detrimental than a party-line or worse, completely arbitrary, vote.

I knew that I wanted to be an educated voter, but I had no idea how to get the information I needed to make an informed decision, so I stayed away from the ballot box.

My belief is that our culture makes it too difficult to find that information, gives us too little time to digest said information, and does not encourage the populace to get out and vote.

And yes, this is important at the local, state and federal levels. Each arena has wide-reaching effects on the people it serves.

Again, I'm not an expert on the topic, but I would like to see more done to fight gerrymandering, to continue to enforce "one person, one vote" programs, to find new and implement tried measures for voter engagement and to encourage our voting populace to vote each and every time there is an election.

For the voting system to work properly, we must all engage and do our part, but we must also have ready access to the information and polling places, with as few obstructions as possible.

I now vote in every election, at the city, state and federal levels, and reward myself with a donut every time, just so I don't forget to celebrate my RIGHT to vote!

ELISSA DAVIS

I graduated from the University of Houston, Summa Cum Laude, with a degree in Hotel and Restaurant Management. After fulfilling my lifelong dream of being a professional chef, I switched gears and started working in retail customer service in the non-profit arena. I am currently the Director of Customer Service and Retail Sales for The Jung Center of Houston. My husband, Mike, is a writer and our cat, Willa, is only getting more beautiful in her old age. We cook together, read together and vote together.

APPRECIATE THE VALUE OF COMPROMISE

> *"Obama's message of yes 'we' can, hinted at the need for a joint effort."*

If I were in charge, the one thing I would do for this country is try to persuade the American people that there is NO ONE SINGLE THING, nor ONE SINGLE PERSON that can make a difference without the support of a community. Change is made through a combination of commitment and compromise and often requires a willingness to forgo personal gain in the interest of society as a whole.

All a U.S. President can do is put forward a sound and robust vision for the country and then work with others to implement that. Simplistic egotistical sound bites get us nowhere. Obama's message of yes 'we' can, hinted at the need for a joint effort. There's no denying that he didn't succeed as well as he might have done in getting that joint effort. It's tough, and it requires the commitment of every single American citizen to support the means to getting to a better society (not just a better life for themselves). JFK's inauguration speech encapsulated the key thought in the 'ask not' quotes. It's not about what your country (or community) can do for you, it's what you can do for your country (or community, or the world – or whatever constituency you choose). Given that we now, unfortunately, do live in a world of sound bites, then I'd initiate an 'Ask Not' campaign with the key objective to get every one of the American people to think about their role in society.

A good place to start would be in the classroom – starting from kindergarten. The campaign doesn't have to be partisan; it could embrace a whole set of topics including history and ethics, that would serve to get everyone thinking about their role and impact as they develop their lives. Hopefully, some of it would rub off onto current political and industry leaders.

PATTI DOSSETT

I am British by birth and a naturalised U.S. citizen. I followed my husband to Houston in 1991, did an MBA at Rice University and pursued a career in strategic marketing. We gave up our home in Houston in December 2015 and are now adjusting to full time life in the UK. There is much to love about American society and certainly I am more appreciative now of the various ways in which people seek to improve their lives and the lives of others – some do see it as an individual responsibility (and act on that responsibility) – others see it as more of a government responsibility (and accept consequent tax and regulatory burdens). I am also more conscious of the numerous examples of economic and social harm that can be done when that individualism is taken too far. And, by the way, neither the UK nor Europe, despite a very different approach to politics, is immune to the same issues!

CREATE UNIVERSAL HEALTH CARE

> *"Millions of people still cannot afford health insurance, especially in the states that refused to expand Medicaid."*

If I were in charge I would create a Universal Health Care system in the United States. Health care has been framed as a privilege rather than a right in this country, and it's time that this outdated framing was shattered. The Affordable Care and Patient Protection Acts of 2010 represented the first major health care reform in the U.S. in almost half a century. For millions of people, over 40 million uninsured, this was a long awaited change that promised to balance the extraordinarily unequal access to health care in this country by allowing more people to purchase affordable insurance, expanding Medicaid, and most importantly, making it illegal for insurance companies to deny benefits to people with pre-existing conditions. It was a needed reform, but it was the wrong policy.

The ACA simply reframed and repackaged privilege. Health care in the U.S. continues to be unjustly rationed by employment, income, insurance, age, race, and citizenship status. Health security, illness prevention, and quality primary care continue to be the privilege of a select few while many individuals and families continue to fall through the cracks of an unjust system, dying of preventable and treatable illnesses. Within this system, health inequities by race and class continue to divide the health of the population, with a majority of the people excluded from access to health care and dying at higher rates from chronic illnesses being historically marginalized black and brown populations. Latinos are currently the most uninsured group in the nation, followed closely by African Americans. Millions of people still cannot afford health insurance, especially in the states that refused to expand Medicaid. Nearly 20 million immigrants were excluded from the 2010 health care reforms based solely on their citizenship status.

The United States spends more of its GDP on health care than any other developed nation, and yet the U.S. population is no healthier for it. Our infant and maternal mortality rate is higher than any other developed nation; we have a lower life expectancy rate and higher rates of obesity, diabetes, and other chronic diseases. It's time for Universal Health Care in United States.

ELIZABETH FARFAN-SANTOS
is an assistant professor of anthropology at the University of Houston. She has a Ph.D. in Medical Anthropology from U.C. Berkeley. Dr. Farfán-Santos' recent book is *Black Bodies, Black Rights: The Politics of Quilombolismo in Contemporary Brazil.* She is working now on the health impacts of political exclusion and institutional discrimination for Latinos disqualified from access to health care and public health resources under current U.S. health care reforms.

HAVE ALL CHILDREN GROW FOOD

> *"Gardening includes math, science and art, even history."*

I never really want to be in charge, but I do have priorities I wish people in charge shared. I feel like education always gets the short stick, and I have one particular passion with regard to education that I would like to see be given much more attention.

There is a love affair with technology. Our kids don't get to experience things tactilely. I want to advocate for a nationwide gardening program at every level. Young people need to know how to grow things and to be outside experiencing nature.

I'd take what Michele Obama has done with her gardening program and just blow it up so that's it's a requirement that kids in school grow food and see how the environment directly impacts us all.

Gardening includes math, science and art, even history. It is about engaging in being alive. I don't understand enough about how to implement national educational policy to tell you just what I would do, but I would figure out how to do something because I believe the benefits are huge.

CAROLYN TOURNEY FLOREK

is a poet, publisher, retired garden designer, and visual artist
who recently moved to Santa Fe, New Mexico after living in Houston,
Texas for more than thirty years. She has a B.S. in Geology (1977) from
Wayne State University, and a B.F.A. in Painting from the University
of Tulsa (1982). Her poetry has been published in *The Texas Review,*
Illya's *Honey*, and several Houston Poetry Fest anthologies, among other
publications. Carolyn's poem, "Over Flat Creek," published in *The Texas
Poetry Calendar 2014*, was nominated for a Pushcart Prize.
She is co-founder with her husband Bob of Mutabilis Press.
Carolyn was Artist-in-Residence at
Bandelier National Monument in fall of 2015.

DELIVER DIGNITY TO THE ELDERLY

> *"It represents our last chance to help them find a modicum of comfort, dignity, and improved sense of well-being."*

Imagine you are in your eighties, subsisting on a modest monthly Social Security check (or a pittance from a local nonprofit); unable to leave your tiny apartment (which is desperately in need of repair to accommodate your increasing infirmities); depressed due to isolation, serious health conditions, and other late life challenges; speak only a few words of English; rarely get visits from family; and your situation worsens in winter when your heater falters, and grows even worse in summer when your home becomes an oven.

Millions of our fellow citizens don't imagine this scenario. They live some variation of it. How can this be? That in a country blessed with so many riches that so many of our elderly live lives of extreme poverty and other forms of deprivation?

If I were in charge, one thing I would do for this country is right this sorry ship. For many of our frail and vulnerable elderly, this is the last stage of what has been a life riddled with desperation and having not; for some, it is a state they have fallen into after a relatively more comfortable life. Either way, it represents our last chance to help them find a modicum of comfort, dignity, and improved sense of well-being.

We could do this by pouring considerably more resources into programs and services that let the elderly not just age in place but do so with dignity, make their lives easier, connect them with their communities, provide meals that not only deliver nutrition but also delight the palette; programs that foster meaningful socialization, learning, and recreation, and that allow older people to share their lifetimes of experience with others, especially the young.

As Hubert Humphrey said, "The moral test of government is how that government treats those who are in the dawn of life, the children; those who are in the twilight of life, the elderly; those who are in the shadows of life; the sick, the needy and the handicapped." Now is the time to ace this test, help this population come out of the shadows and illuminate the twilight.

DICK GOLDBERG

Dick is retired, having been the director of both the Philadelphia and national offices of Coming of Age, an initiative that promotes older adult community engagement. Under his leadership Coming of Age grew from a Philadelphia project to one replicated throughout the country. Because of his pursuing this encore career after age 50 (he had been a successful writer for theatre, film, and TV for 25 years before), he was named one of eighteen 2010 Wells Fargo Second Half Champions. He wrote the off-Broadway drama Family Business, which ran for over a year and was the basis for his becoming a Guggenheim Fellow; authored TV movies and episodes of the TV series Kate and Allie and MacGyver; and wrote book and restaurant reviews for The New York Times and The Philadelphia Inquirer. He holds B.A. and M.F.A. degrees from Brandeis University, where he also taught in the graduate school of theatre arts.

OVERHAUL K-14 EDUCATION

"Everyone will have some practical skills, but not in place of liberal arts."

If I were in charge, I hope I could orchestrate a major overhaul of the pre-collegiate education system. In my vision, free public school would include grades 1-14 so that high school actually absorbs two years of what is now community college. When students graduate at age 20, they are prepared to enter the work force although, of course, they could continue their educations as they wished.

I envision schools running all year round. There would still be three months of vacation, but those vacation days would be interspersed throughout the year so that there is not a three-month lapse. All students stay all fourteen years so that when they graduate, we hope they will have a clearer idea of what they want to do going forward. Everyone will have some practical skills, but not in place of liberal arts.

This program means that drinking, driving and the military are all off bounds 'til age 21 . We stop sending children to war and make it more difficult for them to kill themselves in cars.

Yes, schools will have to change, colleges will have to adapt, camps will have to change but we reduce college debt, absorb vocational training into a system open to all and recognize the changing nature of the world for which young people must prepare.

JOHN T. GOSSETT
was born in Jersey City, New Jersey, then lived in
Clifton, New Jersey and graduated from Clifton High School.
He attended Maryville College in Tennessee.

He danced with Chicago City Ballet with Maria Tallchief Artistic
Director. Since 1983 he has taught Pilates and is
the owner of Pilates Concepts of Houston.
He lives in Houston with his wife and two sons.

PROTECT AMERICAN HOMEOWNERS

> *"I am a person who cares deeply about protecting hard working Americans."*

My attention here is on finance. I find what happened to homeowners in the 2008 mortgage debacle an important lesson about our need for better regulation.

In the thirties, Congress passed the Glass-Stegall Act which established a regulatory separation between traditional banking and higher risk investment activities. Commercial banks could only invest their funds in government bonds or other low-risk instruments. Banks complained that this was unnecessary overregulation that made them less competitive with foreign band. A new bill in the nineties (1999, Graham Leach Bailey Act) repealed the Glass Stegal provisions that stopped FDIC insured banks from taking on riskier investments.

I am not a banker, and I understand there is disagreement about whether Glass Stegal's initial provisions would have stopped the massive collapse of the home mortgages and loss of homes suffered by so many Americans. But I am a person who cares deeply about protecting hard-working Americans. If I were in charge, I would focus intently on creating legislation that would protect American homeowners and community banks from actions that could cause more economic disruption and damage.

I understand that we each have to be responsible for our actions, but it is all too easy to be deceived by untrustworthy individuals who put their own economic gain over truthfulness and full disclosure. Government should put regulatory filters in place that protect the unsophisticated but well-intentioned Americans from predatory business.

⇒·◇·⇐

MICHAEL GREMILLION

was born in a small town in rural Louisiana in 1943. After attending the local parochial grammar school and public high school, Mike graduated from LSU with a degree in physics in 1964. Newlyweds Mike and Ginny moved to Corona, California where Mike worked as a civilian engineer for the Navy for two years before transferring to Houston to work for NASA on the Apollo Program. After Apollo, Mike worked, mostly in software, on various NASA programs until retiring in 1998. Mike was fortunate enough to work very closely with the Astronaut office for most of his 35-year career. Mike and Ginny live in Houston and travel frequently to New Zealand to visit their daughter, son-in-law and granddaughter. Mike and Ginny's son joins them in their annual month-long stay in Paris.

MAKE HEALTHCARE A RIGHT

> *"This would in turn drive down the cost of basic healthcare everywhere."*

I would work to make free access to lifetime preventative and basic healthcare a constitutional "right" for all Americans, regardless of income level, employment status, health status or age. I would strive to make basic healthcare a national ethic and point of national pride, as it is in other countries already. Group and individual health insurance would continue to be available for those who want access to elective and premium healthcare options.

Before ever raising taxes, I would aggressively federally fund expanding medical schools, PA programs and nursing schools to double and triple the supply of more qualified doctors and PAs and nursing professionals, who could then enter the market without the overwhelming burden of crushing student loan obligations. This would in turn drive down the cost of basic healthcare everywhere. This also would overall increase access to preventative and basic healthcare, which in turn reduces long term public healthcare costs and lowers any projected tax burden. I would make certain "states rights" could not trump or waive these basic federal rights.

I would aggressively regulate employer access to pre-employment "drug testing" for non-scheduled substances, such as nicotine (cotinine), pre-employment physicals, pre-employment DNA testing, and use of quasi-legal copies of medical records maintained in non-U.S. databases that waive and overcome the intent of HIPAA regulation.

I would eliminate or make illegal domestic record sharing organizations such as the U.S. Medical Information Bureau, which exists solely to identify "high risk" life insurance candidates, and also exist to deny payment of life insurance policies by parsing and claiming "pre-existing conditions" or other "non-compliance" data that void policy at time of death, even if not related to a claim.

I would destroy the vague meme that "health insurance companies have a right to make a profit," except as they insure elective and premium healthcare policies.

I would make this country a healthier and less scary place to live and work and be well, and I would strive make this policy a point of enthusiasm and national pride.

MICHAEL GRONEWALLER

Currently serving time as a senior executive for a major global technology and consulting firm. Michael is a professional analytics expert and math nerd by day and wild bohemian artiste by night. Michael was born and raised in Germany to a mixed German / American military family. He moved to America at the age of 14, attending Kansas State University on a music scholarship while studying biochemistry in the pre-medicine program. He then moved on to music studies at the Juilliard, and subsequently completed his education in computer science.

Aside from doing math for money, Michael plays both cello and piano, paints in traditional oil in the late renaissance grisaille chiaroscuro style, writes poetry and prose every day, and is an avid fan of applied information theory, algorithmic computer science, artisan bread making and skiing. Although not a medical professional, his personal credo begins with "First, do no harm", which segues nicely into his worldview of striving to be a better humanist, caretaker of the environment and champion for his fellow man.

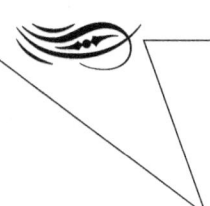

MAKE PHARMACEUTICALS AFFORDABLE
FOR AMERICANS

"Like you just can't gouge people on their health care."

I think our health care system is really broken. The cost for pharmaceuticals is astronomical, and I do think the government should have some sort of control over it so it would be more affordable for everyone in our country and we could all have good health care. As a hair stylist, I have to have an independent policy and my deductibles are sky high. I don't have the same benefits as someone who works in a corporation, and I think I should have that available to me.

It's unfair that there are drugs out there that cost people in our community $1500/ month or more and people in Canada or Mexico can get the same drug for way less. The profit margins are way too high on pharmaceuticals, and there needs to be monitoring. Like you just can't gouge people on their health care. I think there should be an average on deductibles that works for most people.

We now have a system that requires citizens to have health care; and in what was supposed to help everyone, it ended up hurting a lot of us because the deductibles went up. The insurance companies were able to say we'll just raise the deductible and we won't have to spend any more on people. I think we are on the right track but we're just not there yet.

CHERYL GRYDER
is owner of Shine in the Heights salon in Houston, TX.
She has over thirty years in the beauty industry.
She has a B.A. in marketing and advertising
and is a single mom.

COMPULSORY NATIONAL SERVICE
FOR YOUNG PEOPLE

> *"It would open
> eyes, and hopefully
> hearts and minds."*

If I were in charge, one thing I would do for this country is institute compulsory national service for every young person – no exceptions. I am imagining a one-year period where young adults earn minimal wages (enough to live on, in basic conditions) while providing hands-on services in areas such as social work, healthcare, teaching, construction, park maintenance, childcare, technology, conservation efforts, even the military. With so many gaps and shortfalls in this country, the possibilities are truly endless.

In my world, each young person would be required to complete the service prior to his 22nd birthday. I'm drawing on the idea behind the Civilian Conservation Corps, instituted during the Great Depression as a job-creator for the unemployed. Improved national parks and rural roadways were the by-products.

Obviously, the United States would benefit from the talents and manpower provided through this arrangement. In addition, the service would be of great value to the young people themselves. For the privileged and college-bound, the experience would provide a much-needed look into how real life works. It would provide exposure, discipline, and an understanding of the needs within the country. It would open eyes, and hopefully hearts and minds.

For the less fortunate, a year of compulsory service would offer stability, opportunity and perhaps even direction. It would be an alternative to a job at a fast food restaurant, and a place to learn skills, see possibilities, and gain experience.

For those young people lacking clear direction post-high school, a year of service would provide experience, exposure, and – perhaps most valuable – time to think.

I believe a year of mandatory service would create a different context for these young lives going forward. By becoming part of the solution for a brief time, they might become more vested and involved in civic affairs. My belief is also that the satisfaction of having contributed would produce more mature, interesting and aware citizens of the United States.

PAULE SHEYA HEWLETT
is a freelance writer who has specialized in marketing communications for more than 30 years. Her hobby as an artist and textile designer has taken shape as Beyond Her, an artisan line of home and fashion accessories that is sold online and in boutiques.

NON-PARTISAN PRIMARY ELECTIONS

> *"The alternate domination of one faction over another, sharpened by the spirit of revenge . . . is itself a frightful despotism."*

I would work towards non-partisan primaries where all candidates participate in a single unified primary, and the top two candidates go on to compete in the general election.

America is the longest surviving constitutional democracy in the history of the world, and that's because our founders got the structure of government right in drafting the Constitution. But we have had serious difficulties in the last few decades as hyper-partisanship has led to gridlock throughout our political system, undermining Constitutional governance.

George Washington himself understood the danger of this type of partisanship. In his 1796 farewell address, he said that "The alternate domination of one faction over another, sharpened by the spirit of revenge . . . is itself a frightful despotism," and warned that it would ultimately lead people to trust only "in the absolute power of an individual" to the "ruin of Public Liberty."

If I had the power, I would weaken the power of political factions and parties in order to strengthen the will of the people. Non-partisan primaries do just that by having the general election occur between the two most popular candidates in the primary, even if those two candidates come from the same party. This prevents contests which are really decided by a small number of partisan primary voters, and where the general election—with far more voters—is merely a rubber stamp. California has recently adopted this system to good effect.

This may have to occur state by state, but if I were in charge, I would speak out loudly for this change and look for ways to provide federal incentives to encourage states to change. It may seem like a small change, but it would help to get more people elected who represent the political center of their districts rather than the fringes, and who can hopefully work together to help make sure our democracy actually works for all Americans.

JARED HUBBARD
is an appellate and international law attorney born and raised in
Texas, but now based in Newburyport, Massachusetts.
He enjoys long discussions over
drinks on politics and philosophy,
hiking the hills of Scotland, and building
and knocking down block towers
with his two beautiful children.

CREATE JOBS

> *"My interest is on both having jobs and having people ready, willing and able to do the jobs."*

I've thought a fair amount about the question because we have so many priorities as a country, and I think it would be tough to walk into the president's shoes early next year. That said, I've decided that what I would most want to focus on for our country is economic development. Given all the resources we have in the U.S., the unemployment and poverty are shameful to me, and jobs, I believe, are the remedy. So, let's start with job readiness and creation.

The umbrella of economic development is wide ranging so we will have to to consider related policy issues from trade issues and early childhood education to job retraining and equipping our workforce for the available jobs. But my interest is on both having jobs and having people ready, willing and able to do the jobs.

I'm not an economist so I won't comment on the best ways to stimulate job creation. But I do know we have lots of levers at our disposal and we probably need all of them – infrastructure investment, employment education, public/private investment in societal basics, i.e. "teaching a man to fish". I'm convinced there are solutions that work, with examples all over the country that can potentially be leveraged to make headway on this issue given significant attention and resources.

DEBBIE JOHNSON
grew up in Nebraska and graduated from the
University of Nebraska. She did additional advanced coursework
at MIT and with Peter Senge. After a couple decades of working
for AT&T/Lucent Technologies, ending as regional vice president,
she began a career in consulting. Today, she lives with her
family in Austin, TX, consults with companies on
their philanthropic strategies and is board
chair for Leadership Austin.

GIVE ALL CHILDREN COMPUTER SKILLS

> *"It's not enough to talk about making sure all areas of the country are wired for broadband."*

The issue that especially interests me is job displacement in an information society. Advances in technology have created haves who can use the technology and those who don't function well in this domain.

We have already seen the elimination of manufacturing jobs in which routine processing can be done by machines, and routine office work is subject to similar displacement. This is a major shift that affects how people will work. I believe it is an obligation of our government and private institutions to put policies in place that will help prepare a work force ready for the demands of the work place.

We have to make sure that young people, K-12 and beyond, are capable of using computers and comfortable understanding their capacities. It's not enough to talk about making sure all areas of the country are wired for broadband. All children need access to computer training and an introduction to computational thinking.

And if I were in charge, I would discourage the illusion that everyone should have a college education. Everyone should have an education, but we need people educated to be electricians, plumbers and mechanics, roofers and builders. And we need empathetic people in nursing, home care and other service professions, educated to apply interpersonal skills to problems our computers are not going to solve.

Perhaps the community college system is the best place to focus and direct more public funds as an investment in our future. And for those who have difficulty finding a foothold in this era of technological change, universal medical coverage and a base level of material support should be provided as a corrective to the extreme income inequality that now prevails, and jobs programs similar to those created during the Great Depression should be instituted.

DICK KARP

is a theoretical computer scientist. He designs algorithms and studies fundamental limits on the complexity of computation. Born in Boston in 1935, he was educated at Boston Latin School and Harvard University.

Since 1968, except for a four-year interlude in Seattle, he has been at the University of California at Berkeley, where he is currently a University Professor and Director of the Simons Institute for the Theory of Computing. He has a twenty-seven year-old son, and lives in San Francisco with his wife.

IMPROVE THE STUDENT LOAN SITUATION

If I were president of the United States of America, I would tackle issues related to student loans. Student loans is an issue I personally care deeply about, as it has affected me and my family. I understand this is a complex issue, however, I would do everything in my power to try and curb the high interest rates. While I will not graduate college with enormous debt, my older brother has just graduated optometry school two years ago, and is deeply buried in debt. He owes an incredible amount of money and had to take out a loan to cover tuition, housing, and living expenses. At the time (he was 22) he did know about the huge amount of interest he would accumulate at the end of his four years in optometry school.

His quality of life has suffered due to the ridiculously high bills he pays each month to cover his loans. My older brother has not been rewarded well for achieving the American dream due to student loans. While we are taking advantage of the opportunities given to us, we also are being punished for not having money upfront to pay for college. Young men and women should not be afraid to enroll in a respected University because their parents do not have the money to pay for the increasing tuition. Instead, American universities should be accessible to all young people who strive to achieve greatness in life. Student loans with interest is expected; however, we are punishing young men and women with high interest rates for attending a four year college institution, while those with wealthier parents are given an opportunity to attend college with zero debt.

RONAK KARSAN

I am a student at the University of Houston and part of the business honors program. I am currently studying accounting and am striving to work for one of the big four accounting firms after I graduate. My parents came to America in the mid 1980s and owned and operated a motel to make money. Both of them are uneducated, however they always stressed the importance of getting a college education to have a higher standard of living.

Both my siblings and I have seen them struggle financially, and I would like to take full advantage of the opportunities ahead of me to support myself and my parents in the coming years. Now, I am a junior at the University of Houston majoring in accounting.

WORK ON ELECTION REFORMS

> *"The easier we make
> it for people to vote,
> the better I think it is."*

It's so hard to choose just one issue. I'm so fed up with the mess we have made. Ordinarily, I would choose an education issue because it is doable. We are never going to get rid of poverty, but we can make headway with education. But I am going to choose election reform because I think that is also doable.

I would like to go back in time before Citizens United – or go forward and get rid of it. And if we really think about election reform, we have to think about the electoral college and moving to a system where the popular vote is what determines our choice. I worry that this might hurt the two party system in ways that we wouldn't like so I would have to think about that, but the way things are working now troubles me.

And then there's gerrymandering. Congress has got to fix this one. If I could, I would mandate that voting districts didn't have a solid block of any one thing. I'm not sure how you control that geographically since people move and they are likely to move in ways that have likes aggregated. We probably need a rule about what a district can consist of so that geography matters but diversity matters more.

And I like the way here in Texas you can vote early for any reason. The easier we make it for people to vote, the better I think it is. Rules that make it harder, rules that fix problems that don't really exist to make it harder for poorer people to vote, hurt the system and that hurts all of us.

ANN KAUFMAN

is a Houstonian deeply involved in civic affairs.
Ann is especially committed to children and their well-being.
A page-plus list of honors and honors testifies to the skills and
determination she applies to everything with which she is
engages, including her tennis game. Among those awards is
the 2013 Eugene H. Vaughan Civic Leadership Award
from the Center for Houston's Future, the 2006
Kneebone Volunteer of the Year award from the
United Way of Greater Houston, and the
Frank L. Weil Award 2000 from the
Jewish Community Centers of North America.

Ann and her husband Stephen travel widely,
often with their children and grandchildren,
and find life interesting and satisfying.

INSTITUTE RIGOROUS ENVIRONMENTAL POLICIES

"I believe it is not only our right but our responsibility to take action and protect our planet."

I am impressed by the group of 21 young Americans who are suing the U.S. government for failing to create rigorous environmental policies which has resulted in massive climate change and global warming as evidenced by the recent flood in Houston, the second one in two years.

If I were in charge, I would create rigorous environmental policies which aim to reduce greenhouse emissions, water pollution due to fracking and oil spills, and the destruction of the ecosystem due to genetically modified plants. I believe it is not only our right but our responsibility as responsible citizens of the free and prosperous world to take action and protect our planet to ensure that our future generations will thrive.

KULSOOM KISHWAR

I love dancing, writing, hiking,
cooking, and eating. I currently live in
Houston, TX with my partner where I am completing
my degree in Oriental Medicine. I love and cherish
this planet and strive to live my life in accordance with
the natural way. After graduation I am eager to travel,
study Qigong and martial arts, and eventually
practice, teach, and write about Classical
Chinese Medicine and inspire those around
me to protect and live in harmony
with our natural environment.

STAND UP AGAINST INTOLERANCE
AND DEMONIZATION

> *"I would ask all of us to hear the views of those who disagree with us."*

Ihave had so many answers to this question, but the one I keep coming back to seems impossible, and yet it is what I keep thinking we need so badly. I want to wave my magic wand and reduce intolerance in the country. I see nationally and even in my own small academic environment an increasing tendency to demonize people who disagree with us.

Polarization is proliferating, and it causes people to disengage. That leaves the stage open to those not afraid or embarrassed by vindictiveness. As the recent presidential campaign is demonstrating, there seems to be no price and even reward to insult.

I am not arguing against disagreement. I teach in a law school. Of course, I respect differing opinions and believe we need more conversation about our differences, respectful, informed, factual conversations. If I could, I would ask all of us to hear the views of those who disagree with us, whether by reading a different newspaper or blog or listening to oppositional radio or TV.

What I could do is ask leaders at every level of organization from elementary schools to global corporations to call out people who demonize, to stand up in front of those they are leading and ask for a more respectful, thoughtful dialogue. We have accepted recycling, energy efficiency and smoking reduction. I am confident we can learn or re-learn the art of civility as well. If it begins with leaders, it may filter down throughout all sorts of organizations.

Finally, I would push back against "Let's not discuss politics." Shouldn't we be discussing politics as much as celebrity gossip, sports predictions or restaurants?

If I were in charge of the county, I would look for ways to get people to discuss the politics of policy, maybe posting a topic each month with a fact sheet.

ANNE LAWTON
teaches at the Michigan State University Law School. Lawton has been recognized for excellence in teaching and is a respected expert on individual and small business debtors in Chapter 11.

OFFER ALL WOMEN AFFORDABLE, ACCESSIBLE, INFORMED HEALTHCARE

"Reproductive health is the cornerstone of maternal and child health."

My issue is women's health. I'm passionate about making good health care more accessible, available and affordable for women who are disproportionately affected by bad health care.

Reproductive health is the pivotal issue because it is the center of a wheel that affects women, their families and beyond that our national economy. It is the cornerstone of maternal and child health. It affects poverty, education, nutrition and economic development. It impacts on mental health for both mothers and children and even fathers.

When we deny women access to education regarding pregnancy prevention and pregnancy termination, we stand blind to the interconnectivity of what we are doing and how it fans out across lifetimes.

Certainly, I would speak out in support of Planned Parenthoods. Having worked there, I know how much good this organization does for women. Abortions are less than 3% of their services. This is a place where woman receive health check ups, find out about pregnancy prevention and are treated with respect and dignity regardless of their income or color. If I were in charge, I would figure out ways to make such services more accessible.

We squander our human resources when we undervalue the well being of women in this country, and whoever is in charge has a responsibility to do all she can to unleash everyone's full potential.

MARY JO LAZEAR
spent 14 years as a director of
Planned Parenthoods and then worked on women's
health programs in 14 countries in Europe and Eurasia.
Since then, she has worked as a consultant specializing
in executive transitions, strategic planning and
board/staff relationships for non-profits.

IMPROVE REFUGEE RESETTLEMENT

"Welcome the victims and community members who have been impacted by this devastating crisis."

One of my top issues is resettlement. In light of the current refugee crisis worldwide, my interest in this issue spans quite a number of topics, including education, immigration, infrastructure and development.

What would I do if I were in charge? I would bring an end to the conflict in the Middle East, negotiate peace talks, rebuild where political, social, cultural systems have been marred by this conflict. I would collaborate to create new processes and systems in Europe and around the world to welcome the victims and community members who have been impacted by this devastating crisis. There is no easy fix and no set solution; I would love to be a part of the solution. I am also passionate about the current refugee crisis; it has been considered the worst migrant crisis since World War II. There has been an impact on Europe and other neighboring countries. Syrians have been amongst the most affected. For countries who have faced infrastructural strain of welcoming refugees who are fleeing violence in the Middle East, only 10% of Syrian refugees have fled to Europe; there has been little in preparation for this influx of migrants. Overall, 13.5 million Syrians require humanitarian assistance, 6.6% of whom are internally displaced within Syria and over 4.8 million who have fled the country.

Each year, the United States allows 70,000 refugees from all over the world to enter the country annually. This year, the Obama administration has allowed another 15,000 Syrian refugees to immigrate to the U.S with a total of 85,000 refugees for the fiscal year. Moreover, the United States continues to be the largest single humanitarian donor to provide millions for the world's most vulnerable people around the world with lifesaving assistance through the State Department's Bureau of Population, Refugees and Migration (RPM). Though the United States is a large economic contributor to assist and alleviate this migratory crisis, there are still more beneficial changes and sustainable solutions overseas and domestically that are needed to provide aid for this issue.

CHRISTINE LIBOON

I am a homegrown born and raised San Diegan. I grew up in Chula Vista, California and am a first-generation born Filipino-American who considers herself a global citizen. I earned my B.A. in Ethnic Studies from the University of California, Riverside. I enjoy outdoor sports including rock-climbing and hiking. I also practice yoga. I am looking to continue to further my education in Research, International Development and Education.

I am currently working in the humanitarian sector as a Vocational ESL Teacher with the International Rescue Committee, one of the largest resettlement agencies. I work with newcomers, particularly refugees, SIVs (Special Immigration Visa holders) and asylees.

Previously, I worked with TIDES (Transformative Inquiry Designs for Educational Systems) as an office administrator and assistant as well as a web moderator. I also spent time as a field researcher with TIDES on the MALDEF project and worked in Spain as a Language Teacher and assistant under the Spanish Ministry of Education.

ONE NATIONAL EDUCATION LAW
TO SERVE ALL CHILDREN

> *"Children are the world's most valuable resource and its best hope for the future."*

If I were in charge, one thing I would do for this country is to restore our nation's children and their right to a globally enviable public education to an exalted place on our domestic policy agenda.

I would quote and repetitively re-quote President John F. Kennedy: "Children are the world's most valuable resource and its best hope for the future." I would go on and quote President John Adams, who in 1785 said, "The whole people must take upon themselves the education of the whole people and be willing to bear the expenses of it. There should not be a district of one mile square, without a school in it, not founded by a charitable individual, but maintained at the public expense of the people themselves."

I have an intractable belief in "public" education and in children, every single one and from every race, nationality, wealthy to economically disadvantaged and from gifted to with disabilities. Every child would matter. Every child would be offered a globally enviable public education and would be counted as one of America's children and not the property of fifty states and 14,000 plus school districts and a non-regulated free-for-all-profit-guzzling charter school system.

If I were in charge I would go to Congress and convince Democrats Republicans and our populace that our nation's school-age children are "purple." They are not born "red" or "blue." They belong to all of us and have never been served under local control. We would carry on President Lyndon B Johnson's 1965 Elementary-Secondary Education Act and dream of an equitable education for all children and with a teaching force to match.

America has had two federal K-12 education laws. The Elementary-Secondary Education Act (poorly rebranded the No Child Left Behind and now newly branded, Every Student Succeeds Act) was signed into law in 1965 and the Education for all Handicapped Children's act, (renamed the Individuals with Disabilities Education Act) was signed in 1975. These federal laws have yet to deliver their promise of an equitable public education for EVERY child. I would drive ONE LAW that says, for everyone to hear, that every child has value and matters equally in the United States.

MARCIE LIPSITT

lives in Michigan with her husband, son and three dogs. She was born feeling the ills, pain and prejudice that plagued children like her sister with severe learning disabilities and brother with ADHD; a father with Bipolar Disorder and OCD and frankly any child who appeared to have a challenge. She stood up for the kids in school being made fun of. Little did she realize she was evolving advocacy and activism skills. For the past 25 years she has been a mother to her greatest inspiration and hero, her son Andrew. Andrew has severe learning disabilities and including NLD, PDD-NOS,CAPD and EFD but in addition he suffers from the childhood onset of Bipolar Disorder, OCD, ADHD, multiple anxiety disorders and medical morbidities.

Currently, Marcie is the founder and co-chair of the Michigan Alliance for Special Education and a persistent advocate for children who are poorly served by our schools and our communities. In 2011, Marcie attended the first William & Mary Law School, Institute for Special Education Advocacy. In October 2013 became one of the first to graduate from the inaugural Council of Parent Attorney and Advocates ("COPAA"), Special Education Advocacy Training ("SEAT") program, and is nationally recognized as an advocate with advanced training.

REQUIRE LIABILITY INSURANCE
FOR GUN OWNERS

> *"No other industry regulates
> our lives more than insurers."*

The right to bear arms described in the second amendment seems to have become a "third rail" in politics – something whose touch is liable to kill you politically. The financial reach of the NRA has made it difficult for politicians to stand up to the NRA, even when the majority of their constituents – from both parties – favor some sort of limitation on the sale of arms. When you couple this with 13,286 people being killed by firearms during 2015 (BBC News), we are faced with an enormous challenge.

All of this is compounded by new carry laws. Besides concealed carry options, there are some states allowing the open carrying of firearms (even shot guns) in public places. With 300 million guns in the country, and little regulation, it is scary to think of how many armed folks may be walking around Target when I go shopping next time.

If I were in charge, I would advocate for a simple solution that would not pressure politicians to vote against guns. Simply: I want liability insurance required for all guns.

We are required to have liability insurance for our automobiles, the other potentially lethal weapon most of us own. Every state requires some form of liability coverage, usually called "bodily injury" for all motor vehicles. In order to register a car, we must provide proof of this coverage. Why not guns too?

No other industry regulates our lives more than insurers. They want to know the height of fencing around pools, speed of a golf cart, how many seat belts in a car, etc. Just imagine the requirements for insuring a gun! They might include how the gun is stored, who has access, initial and continued training of the owner, number and age of children in the home, and whether anyone in the dwelling has mental illness. Just as auto insurers want to know how many miles we drive, gun insurance would likely want to know how and when the gun will be used.

Even if "we the people" were able to convince Congress to stand up to the NRA, I would still propose that all guns carry liability insurance. The establishment of insurance requirements would work toward reducing the thousands of lives lost to guns each year. Surely a gun is as potentially dangerous as my street legal golf cart?

BJ (ELIZABETH) MCCONNELL
has lived across the United States but currently plays golf with
her newly retired husband in Jupiter Florida. BJ worked in the
field of prevention and wellness for forty years. She created programs
and training for teachers and law enforcement nationwide.
She is the mother of two and grandmother of three.

SYSTEMATIZE ENVIRONMENTAL REFORMS

"Every human will need to be committed if we are going to be successful."

I might have to be in charge of the world to pull this off...

I would reach out to each major industrial country to form a cross-disciplined scientific committee. The challenge of that committee is to a) identify the environmental issues that are in need of addressing, and b) prioritize them in order of importance. This global effort will have national, regional, state, city, neighborhood sub-committees monitoring the challenges.

This prioritized list would then be given to a global, cross-functional team who would develop the implementation plan; that plan would need to be broken down to its smallest parts — in languages, cultures, etc. — as every human will need to be committed if we are going to be successful. Whatever is at the top of the list would be addressed first (carbon?), etc. Clearly there would be some things that could be addressed simultaneously, but the committee would monitor the state of the success/failure and ensure that no mission-critical issue is allowed to derail the process. Successes will be celebrated along the way and saving the environment and our earth will be our universally shared challenge.

Industrialized countries would bear the responsibility (educationally and financially) for developing countries. Clearly developing countries will have to collaborate closely so that the training/changes/buy-in succeeds.

I choose this as my top priority because if we cannot sustain healthy life on earth, nothing else we do matters.

MARY MCCOY

is a career transition expert. She provides job-search optimization for clients who are between jobs and assists others in identifying a career path that will be more fulfilling. A former senior vice president of human resources, Mary leverages her understanding of the corporate world to enhance her effectiveness.

Mary's career took a turn for the adventurous when she fulfilled a life-long dream to work on an island in the Pacific. What was supposed to be a two-year project turned into a ten-year experience of a lifetime in the Kingdom of Tonga in the South Pacific.

Mary has been a regular contributor to Forbes.com. She has a Masters degree in Human Behavior from United States International University and an undergraduate degree in psychology from Saint Mary's College, Notre Dame, IN.

DEATH WITH DIGNITY, DEATH WITH CHOICE

> *"In the past social reforms have eventually overridden institutional prejudices and dogma."*

If I were in charge, one thing I'd do for the country is to initiate universal and competent hospice care for the dying and include the right to access aid in dying for mentally competent terminally ill adults who request it. I would model this physician assisted dying law after the Oregon Death with Dignity Act where it has been successfully regulated since 1997 with proven safe guards to protect patients. Each state would implement this law as Oregon has implemented theirs.

Institutional opposition to aid in dying prevents the majority of Americans from gaining access to this end of life care. In the past social reforms have eventually overridden institutional prejudices and dogma. Slavery was ended as an accepted practice; women obtained the right to vote in most countries, and civil rights laws were passed ending legal discrimination against minorities. Compassion towards others in need drove these changes.

Providing an avenue to a gentle and humane death for those patients undergoing hopeless suffering towards an inevitable death allows peace of mind for those patients choosing this voluntary option.

CINDY MERRILL, J.D., is a graduate of The George Washington University in Washington, D. C. and obtained her law degree in 1984 from South Texas College of Law in Houston, Texas. She is formerly an assistant district attorney in Harris County and was Chief Prosecutor of its Family Criminal Law Division for 13 years.

Ms. Merrill was recognized by The Houston Post and Texas Executive Women as one of the top ten 1993 "Women on the Move" and the recipient of the 1995 Toby Myers Statewide Leadership Award. She received the 1989 Community Service Award and the 1995 Women's Suffrage Award from the Houston Area Women's Center and was honored in 1993 by the local chapter of the National Council on Jewish Women as a Woman of Influence.

In 2013, along with Ms. Penny Shelfer, Ms. Merrill founded Texas Death with Dignity which educates citizens on end of life issues through presentations, its Facebook page, website, opinion articles and media interviews. It advocates for an aid in dying statute in Texas.

REDIRECT OUR FUNDING

*"So little money
is going into ensuring
that the future of our country
remains sustainable."*

If I were in charge, I would drastically change the funding policy that the federal government currently has implemented so that less money is put into war and more money is put into bettering our social infrastructure within our country and creating better relationships with other countries. So little money is going into ensuring that the future of our country remains sustainable. A small fraction of governmental funds is going into education, science, healthcare, while the majority is going into short term goals that will only distance ourselves from other countries.

Many people in America are too driven by social stigmas about other countries and refuse to step out of that man-made boundary and work together to better each country. These stigmas are created by a lack of knowledge of other countries, sparking a sort of fear of the unknown if America works with them. So many phrases of propaganda are associated with different countries, to where we completely ignore them, shut them out, or oppress them – Mexico: "They're taking our jobs," Iraq: "They're terrorists," Finland: "They're socialists." We need to break down those man-made borders and see them as no different than we.

So much money is going into creating borders between one another, rather than collaborating to make sure the best policies are being made for each country. We are falling behind in education, one of the most important resources we could possibly have, which has the power to guarantee our future success, because not enough attention is going towards it. Why continue to broaden our tensions by tackling issues with more issues? It's completely counterproductive. We have so many resources that the government barely bats an eye at, but are crucial to ensuring a continual progress of our country. If we really want to "make America great again", then we have to tackle the issues that have been ignored, and stop feeding into the issues that are holding us back.

Hello world. My name is **ANTHONY MOORE**
(I usually go by Tony). I'm from Houston, Texas.
I've played violin for 12 years so far. I'm currently a biochemistry
major and part of the Honors College at the University of Houston.

I'm a co-founder of an organization called
Honors in Community Health and
current internal coordinator.
I'm also a really avid dog person.

INCREASE AFFORDABLE ACCESS TO
HIGH QUALITY EDUCATION

> *"If you have the money, you can buy an outstanding education."*

I grew up in Germany and earned my high school and college degrees there. My Ph.D. training is from Germany and Princeton University, funded by fellowships, mostly from Germany. Not only my career as a scientist but my whole life has been shaped by this education. It provides me with more than an economic foundation for my life. It is the essence of what I am today. It has given me great joy and opened my mind to the wonders of the world. And it was free. In Germany, education is free for all students.

I now live in the United States and appreciate the dynamic culture of science here, the incredible opportunity to realize your imagination if you dare to try, which is not without risk but with a much higher chance for success than in Europe. But now comes the big IF. The IF is IF you can afford it. The incredible education one can obtain in the USA comes at a price. If you have the money, you can buy an outstanding education. If not, you might still get lucky, but luck favors only a few. In the U.S. there is a wonderful commercial marketplace in which parents can buy opportunity for their children. Some students gain both the joy of knowledge and the skills to a good economic life while others have little chance of gaining either.

I am not a socialist, but there must be an alternative to the path of social separation that is driven in the USA by the education system that is resulting in an increasingly polarized society. The risk is not just social polarization but also intellectual poverty for a large part of the society and missed economic opportunity for the country.

It may be hard for a U.S. citizen to believe that the quality of life is better elsewhere, but I am seeing foreign men and women who are trained here leave for countries with more interesting opportunities and a chance for a better life. Why not live where your struggle is less – in part because you do not have to pay the very high costs to educate your kids and pay for their healthcare? I think a reform of the USA education system is an incredibly difficult but necessary goal. Yes, it will face fearful opposition much like the healthcare reform because many financial interests are at stake. Our commercialized education system is making the USA a less interesting and desirable place to be. If I were in charge, I would do all I could to create more opportunities with less cost.

ULIRICH (ULI) MUELLER
works on the molecular mechanisms of auditory perception.
He has recently served as the Director of the Dorris Neuroscience
Center at Scripts Research Institute in La Jolla and begins now as
Bloomberg Distinguished Professor of Neuroscience and Biology at
Johns Hopkins University in Baltimore. He is married to a scientist,
and they are parents of two daughters.

CONSIDER A REPARATIONS BILL
AND REDUCE RACIAL INEQUALITY

> *"Not learning about other races gives us very little to draw from as a society."*

If I could do one thing for this country, I would address the issue of racial injustice. Race has proven to be one the most divisive characteristics in our society, and most of the history of race in this country is negative. This is extremely unfortunate, because we live in such a diverse country that being able to draw from a wide range of viewpoints could and should be used to our advantage. Instead, race division has served as a hindrance, which has kept many groups separated and thereby not able to learn from one another.

I believe one of the best places to address racism would be by integrating all cultures into the primary and secondary school curriculum. Currently, the school curriculum seldom mentions people of color, and when it does, it is generally how they related to Europeans. Not learning about other races gives us very little to draw from as a society and leaves us very susceptible to negative racial stereotypes that we may learn from other sources, like the media. Whereas, on the opposite end of the spectrum, we learn many positive attributes about those of European descent and have positive images to draw from to dispel any negative stereotypes.

With regards to the injustice that has been caused by racism, it is difficult to truly examine the extent without a proper assessment. As a result, there should be serious consideration of the study of reparations bill that has been proposed by Congressman John Conyers since 1989, which would determine what actions would help resolve issues that have resulted from decades of racial inequality.

If we could properly address the issue of race, we could solve many other similar issues regarding disenfranchised communities, like those marginalized by their religion or sexual orientation. This will only take place though if we stop using racial division for causes like political gain and focus on empowering the lives of all of our fellow citizens.

DANYAHEL (DANNY) NORRIS
is a law school instructor/administrator
and an intellectual property attorney.
He can be found on
Twitter @ danorris007.

REDEFINE LEADERSHIP

"Leadership involves both standing alone and listening to others."

In November I will vote for the ninth time for President. I find myself alarmed by the choices – surely, someone should be a standout for me, someone I'm excited about voting for. Instead, I'm worried about the ramifications of electing any of them as leader of the free world.

And so I dream about what one thing I would do if I were in charge – lead. General Douglas MacArthur said, "A true leader has the confidence to stand alone, the courage to make tough decisions, and the compassion to listen to the needs of others. He does not set out to be a leader but becomes one by the equality of his actions and the integrity of his intent." Notice that leadership involves both standing alone and listening to others. It involves compassion and integrity. How do we get this kind of leadership?

I would eliminate caucuses and legislate open primaries. Let's do away with super delegates and Super PACs. Let's have electoral districts drawn independently. Let's rotate the order of state voting. Elections should be based on popular vote exclusively. When leaders are truly elected BY THE PEOPLE, it increases the chances that a President can have genuine confidence that s/he can spend his/her days in office leading. That must include working with the other party (or parties, if we could be so lucky), and even having the confidence to appoint people of other political persuasions to the Cabinet. There is far too much cronyism and political posturing now.

A real leader would know that s/he must devote time and energy to making sure Congress works together to find middle ground whenever possible, instead of rejoicing over their ideological differences and standing ground needlessly – the end result being stagnation and division. Congress has turned into a bunch of willful, spiteful children, and we now need the firm hand of a real leader to make them WANT to work together. Collaboration is the hallmark of democracy. It's been sorely lacking in all political arenas and it's what a real leader would strive to accomplish.

HEATHER J. PERLMUTTER
is currently a Portfolio Manager at
Tocqueville Asset Management L.P. with a focus
on both taxable and tax-exempt fixed income.

Ms. Perlmutter earned a B.A. in Communication
from Rutgers University in 1986.
She lives in New York City with her
husband and two children.

WE NEED FULL EMPLOYMENT

> *"We may begin to see more responsive corporate governance and more creativity with inventions as well."*

If I were in charge, one thing I would do for this country is return America to full employment for ALL with maximized education, values of peace and harmony, respect for the environment, support of our elders and children and balanced corporate profits to ensure creativity. This is an America The Beautiful.

I grew up on a 110 acres rice, cotton, corn and cattle farm in South Texas. Memories of all workers and farm owners 'pulling' together to ensure the best outcome each season and sharing the financial rewards of the results ensured my family years of adequate income for our family and the workers. Today it is the absence of 'pulling' together or lack of trust at a basic level which hinders today's America The Beautiful.

My prediction is that full employment will unleash in America's citizenry increased participation in local, state and national elections. This increase will support more 'pulling' together and ensure a different message among candidates vying for elections and different kind of participation once men and women are elected. They will REALLY represent the people rather than selfish interests or high dollar political Pac control. We may begin to see more responsive corporate governance and more creativity with inventions as well. Finally, another outcome of a majority of citizens participating may well be an increase in more national and local peace and harmony – we will all become citizens and not have disparate groups as fearful citizens. In conclusion, if all Americans see and have hope of participating in OUR country, we gain the human capital potential of the richness of all citizenry.

LILLIAN PETTY

I am age 69 (DOB 1/23/1947), an African American of
the Christian faith. I work as a population
health consultant.

CULTIVATE STILLNESS

> *"... breathing, meditating, painting, playing an instrument, reading, writing, praying, or something else."*

I have never considered myself to be a "political" person, so what I write here might be off point in the context of a heated political year. My first instinct is to say, "Do no harm" (does that make me a doctor, or a Libertarian?). It seems, though, that for many in our Congress especially, being "in charge" means not so much as doing no harm, but doing nothing at all, except obstructing the business and responsibilities of governing. Ok, then, now that I've gotten that off my chest, what would I do?

I would ask each of us, current candidates for president included, for at least fifteen minutes each day, to cultivate stillness. The definition of that might mean breathing, meditating, painting, playing an instrument, reading, writing, praying, or something else. In short, taking some quiet time to reflect and taking a break from the sniping, squabbling, spinning, barking, tweeting, messaging, posturing and posing that seem to have become daily staples of our media saturated and so-called "socially connected" lives. Perhaps, if each of us took this time, each of us would be prompted to consider what it is that really matters, and we could project that consideration unto others. Maybe in that stillness we could each find a common thread, a decency of humanity, that binds all of us together in a more loving and compassionate way.

JOE PIROPATO
is a portfolio manager at Toqueville Asset Management in NYC.
A summa cum laude graduate of Princeton where he majored
in renaissance history, Piropato is also involved in running
a charitable foundation for the arts, advising a web-based
interview series of well-known classical musicians
and providing board leadership for the International Festival
Society which makes grants to young American musicians and
composers. He continues to study and play the piano.

HELP MORE STUDENTS STAY IN SCHOOL AND DO WELL

> *"Children need to be taught the importance of school and why they are there."*

I was born in 1996 in the suburbs of Chicago and was raised by two Mexican American parents who both emigrated from Mexico. I moved to Houston at the age of six and found myself behind my current grade's reading level. I graduated high school in 2014 with a GPA and class rank I was not very proud of, and while every student was getting acceptance letters to big name universities, I stuck with community college. However, I was the first male in both of my parents' families to graduate high school and not go into carpentry or begin full-time at a dead-end job with a GED, although my older sister attended college before I did.

I've seen cousins and friends drop out of high school because they were lazy or not smart enough; some had family or financial problems outside of school or just did not have the resources in general. If I were in charge, I would want to change education. President Obama has his 'Higher Education' plan to increase school standards and assessments, but not every student has the resources to attend school and stay in school. I think more schools should be built, there should be increased access to bus transportation for students, and better courses should be given.

Children need to be taught the importance of school and why they are there; this needs to be taught early on and reminded constantly. Middle school and early high school students need to be prepared for college, and from my experience, there was not enough help in applying to universities, scholarships or financial aid, or even knowing what to expect after graduation. I think there should be a better tracking system on how a student is doing and how ready he or she is for the next steps.

Creating more schools will not only benefit the students, but will create more jobs. Of course there will be construction contracts, plumbing, technology contracts, etc., but there will also be more teachers and faculty, more bus drivers, janitors, and school dietitians. Families in need require cheaper, more accessible school supplies; more organizations and shelters for the homeless should have access to these supplies as well. Not only should schools be accountable, but the parents as well; there should be stricter fines when it comes to student absences and faults of that nature.

ROBERT RODRIGUEZ
is a junior at the University of Houston
pursuing a BBA in Management Information Systems.

CHALLENGE AMERICANS TO REACH FOR THE STARS

> *"I would challenge America to reach for the stars."*

As a child of the 1960s, I remember firsthand how landing a man on the moon sent American optimism into the stratosphere. As terrifying a time as it was – between assassinations, riots and the television coverage of the war – we saw the pinnacle of American ingenuity. There was nothing we could not do.
Of course there were naysayers, detractors who said it would never work, it was too expensive, a colossal waste of time. But this one time, we pushed them aside and achieved something great. The resulting technologies inspired a generation of scientists, spawned entirely new industries and changed the lives of millions of people forever.

But time passed. The Soviets, our rivals in the race to the moon, no longer seemed interested so we lost interest. Decades of conservatism succeeded in limiting our boundless enthusiasm, because at the end of the day conservatism is about limits. The naysayers who told us it was too expensive seized control of the purse strings and starved our space program. Great nations engage in great public works. They define our culture and our national identity. The Egyptians knew that; the Romans knew that; and we marvel at the things they left behind. What will future generations marvel about America?

NASA is designing the next generation of rockets for a manned mission to Mars. The plan is to go out, plant the flag and come back. We should be planning to stay there. Our future as a species depends on getting off this planet. There can be no greater accomplishment. Kennedy reminded us in his man on the moon speech that the exploration of space would go on, whether we join or not. It was true then and it is no less true today.

RICHARD ROMAN

has recently reinvented himself as a technology professional in the enterprise resource planning sector. His past lives include being a Navy Supply Corp Officer aboard the USS Enterprise, an administrator for Federal Courts, a corporate trainer and supply chain consultant in both the pharmaceutical and aerospace industries, an entrepreneur and business owner.

He spent his childhood as a military dependent during the Viet Nam war and his teenage years working on the family farm. Both experiences sparked a keen interest in government policy and how the decisions of some people can profoundly affect the lives of others.

He holds a double degree from Gonzaga University in Communications and Business Management and an MBA from the University of Texas at Austin.

THINK GLOBALLY AND STRATEGICALLY

> *"I am convinced
> that my future, and that
> of my grandchildren, is
> intricately connected with
> what happens globally."*

When I considered what I could accomplish if I were in charge, I focused on issues that have always been important to me: women's health and opportunity, climate change, terrorism, education. But I realized that in order to make any difference in these problems, we would need to understand that all these issues are directly affected by the global economy.

We are ethnocentric, worrying only about what is happening in our immediate realm. We neglect to stay current with what is going on with the European Union and the IMF, much less with Third World countries dealing with economic and social devastation. Yet, I am convinced that my future, and that of my grandchildren, is intricately connected with what happens globally. The increase of disease from poor sewage disposal, the development of terrorists from young people with no work and no hope, the impact of pollution from industries that cannot afford to improve safety in factories: all these will come to impact us personally. I am also certain that a better life can be had by the world's poorest, and, as a result, the better will be those in the higher rungs of society.

If I were in charge, I would want our country to look beyond short term disruptions and expenses to the longer strategies. I would encourage the younger generation to study these issues with a broader, more personal, view of the word and its peoples. Most of all, I would call upon experts, but not just those with a Western viewpoint.

LYNN PRESTON ROSAS M.D.
is a recently retired gynecologist who now
has more time to spend with family and friends,
and to pursue more knowledge.

GIVE WOMEN MORE CENTRAL ROLES

> *"Let love
> lead the way
> to put aside
> our
> differences..."*

I think it is time to forward towards a matriarchal approach or administration. We start by acknowledging the contributions of what men have given as far as development is strength. Now is the time for nurturing, caring and management and stabilization that I feel only women can provide. The concerns that plague our country are from the lack of love for not only individuals and their welfare but the earth as well. We are all one.

I feel policy and administration lack a "right" brain approach. Decisions need to be made holistically, taking into account all who benefit and suffer and not writing off one or another regardless of background, culture and socio economic status.

We have come a long way, but we may become lost if we do not strive for balance. Science has proven and disproven old theories that no longer serve us. Let us not be afraid to take a leap that we intuitively know we need. We all want CHANGE!... BIG CHANGES! That change is a matriarchal love for our society, people and planet. In the words of the Beatles " All We Need Is Love." Let love lead the way to put aside our differences and bring forth a newfound strength and leadership that the world could follow together collectively and consciously.

VALENTINE ST. MARTIN

I am a Khemetic Monk. Creator of the Anu Ra Gong System, which means "cultivating heavens light."

I was raised in New York City and attended the University of Southern California.

I am currently working on a book of internal disciplines and strategies for self-evolution, titled after the system that I teach, "Anu Ra Gong."

LET STATES DETERMINE MINIMUM WAGES

> *"No one suggests that $7.25 is a decent living wage."*

Way back in 1967 our politicians and bureaucrats decided that the minimum wage should be $1.40/hr. It wasn't long before the same group decided to up the total. This same gang found this so popular that they raised the rate seven times up to $7.25/hour now. There is enormous pressure to once again raise the minimum wage. The usual prospects have come up with $10.10/hour. Even before the new amount will have been established, they are now proposing $15/hour.

The pros and cons for this idea are as follows:

Pros: Zero

Cons:

1. Students and young inexperienced people will have little chance of getting an entry-level job.

2. Small businesses will be most affected. Some will go broke or close down. Others will raise prices.

3. U.S. industry, already not competitive, will become even less competitive: U.S. industries will continue to leave to Mexico, Asia, or Africa.

No one suggests that $7.25 is a decent living wage. A small number of jobs actually pay such a salary. But every worker making between $7.25 or $10.10 or $15.00 will necessarily have catch-up raise increases. This will be an enormous expense, particularly to small businesses.

There seems to be no way to stop our politicians and bureaucrats. If they thought about it, the solution to the minimum wage discussion is unbelievably simple. One thing I would do for the country is to remove the national minimum wage and let each state set a rate in any way they wish. Problem solved! QED

TOM SCHMIDT

I am a 90-year-old retired man. I grew up in Mexico City
where I owned and managed my own company.
I also worked many years for the IRS
when I moved to the United States. Married
with six children and six grandchildren.

RECOGNIZE THE CRITICAL IMPORTANCE
OF CLIMATE CHANGE ACTION

> *"It is
> probably the
> most dire
> issue facing
> all of us."*

If I were in charge of the country, I would consider it malfeasance not to have climate change at the top of my agenda. It is probably the most dire issue facing all of us. But no substantive change can happen until the campaign finance system is reformed. Political funding has become legalized bribery. The advantages for donors are too easy and too great for them not to exploit. It is the gateway to all the other issues.

In rare instances, the actual will of the people claims a victory, as with Net Neutrality at the FCC last year. But it requires enormous organization and the support of powerful interests facing competing industries (e.g. Google vs. Time Warner). And this reform effort nearly lost! Until the interests of broad cross sections of Americans are considered more important than the narrow interests of electoral politics, we will face a discouraging future.

JACK SKELLEY

is an award-winning writer/editor with expertise in real estate, development, luxury brands, urban design and architecture. Skelley has over 25 years of experience from Harper's magazine to The Atlantic to Los Angeles Times, and is former Executive Editor and Associate Publisher of Los Angeles Downtown News. Skelley currently contributes to Huffington Post, Form magazine, The Architect's Newspaper, and the Modern Luxury family of magazines. Skelley is a frequent planner and moderator of policy forums. He serves on the Advisory Board of Urban Land Institute Los Angeles and is a long-time contributor to Urban Land magazine.

FOCUS MORE ON REHABILITATION
AND LESS ON INCARCERATION

"Surely we have the intellect and will to substitute rehabilitation services and job training for much of confinement."

If I could change anything I would make our criminal justice system more about justice and rehabilitation and less about punishment and shame.

Two years ago criminal justice would never have made my list. I had lived a life that had no exposure to that system and assumed that those convicted were criminals and that what we were inflicting was, indeed, justice. That all changed in October, 2014, when my 22 year-old son was arrested and sent to prison. In the intervening two years, I have seen with my own eyes the disarray and disastrous effects of our criminal justice system.

We've all heard the statistics – the U.S., a beacon of commercial, intellectual, and social leadership, has the highest incarceration rate in the world; with only 5% of the world's population, we lock-up 24% of the world's prisoners. I have come to believe that we are using courts and jails as a way to delude ourselves that we are addressing and solving our country's important societal problems. I do think that people need to be held accountable for serious criminal activity, especially where there are victims. But I believe the prisons are full of young men and women with mental problems, including drug addiction, who need help not punishment. So many of those incarcerated have never been given a chance at education because they are living in poverty or in homes where abuse is rampant.

I have also come to believe that the system is socially and racially biased. My son, who is white and educated, has been treated differently and much better than others in his cellblock. Because I could hire a lawyer and write a letter to the prosecutor, my son got a five-year sentence (in a plea bargain) while the poorer and non-white in his cellblock, who had done exactly the same thing, got anywhere from 12 to 20 years. I'm thankful but outraged. When I visit my son, I see so many families with young children visiting their fathers, and I wonder about the generational impact of this experience. I am heartbroken, and again, outraged. In an age of massive data analytics and sophisticated target marketing – surely we could be more strategic and effective. Surely we have the intellect and will to substitute rehabilitation services and job training for much of confinement. It would cost the same and the return – in terms of lives and treasure – would be so much greater.

EVA ARCHER-SMITH
is a highly sought after Executive Coach who
works with corporate leaders a
round the world.

LINK TAX PREFERENCES TO COMPETITIVE PRACTICES

"The government would have to rescind a windfall tax break if the regulators determine that it poses an unfair advantage over other companies."

In lieu of an "I Have a Dream"-type response, here's a specific, practical example of an initiative waiting to be taken. As president, I would direct the antitrust enforcement division of the Department of Justice and/or the Federal Trade Commission to link tax preferences to competition policy. In other words, the government would have to rescind a windfall tax break if the regulators determine that it poses an unfair advantage over other companies. This strategy has already been adopted by the European Commission and its giving Google, Anheuser Busch, and many others total fits. Tough beans!

This policy builds logically on President Obama's commendable moratorium on inversions. The beauty of it is that private sector companies – those competing with corporations that are getting the tax boons – would support it. In fact, the European Commission was in part driven to its linkage policy by Microsoft, which doesn't want competitors unduly enriched. So it would be hard for a right wing Congress or court to make a case of regulatory over-reaching.

≡⊳◆⊲≡

LARRY SMITH
is a Senior Vice President at LEVICK,
a global crisis communications and PR firm.
He is also a widely published fiction writer.
Visit larrysmithfiction.com

END HUNGER FOR CHILDREN AND ADULTS

"I believe that next to water and air, access to food to thrive is a given right, not a privilege."

Many years ago I was a volunteer for The Hunger Project. The project had three premises: Hunger exists. It doesn't need to. You can make a difference. As a volunteer speaker I learned about the Infant Mortality Rate (IMR) of children dying before the age of one year and how that was linked to poverty and hunger. I also learned that in some cities in the U.S., the IMR was as high as in developing countries. I was stunned!

Later, I volunteered at a local organization that feeds people with life threatening diseases who are at critical nutritional risk. I learned that some of the recipients were sharing their food with their children, who were hungry. This compromised the health of the critically ill person, so MANNA now also provides meals for their children. Again, I was stunned.

As a nutrition educator, I believe that next to water and air, access to food to thrive is a given right, not a privilege. Thus, if I could change one thing in this country, it would be to make sure that every single child and his or her parents do not go hungry for even one day. In a country where obesity is rampant, where we have more than four times the amount of food required by the nutritional needs of our populations, and where much of the food grown is discarded because it is "ugly" and won't sell in the marketplace. We have citizens who are overweight and undernourished. I find the fact that children go to bed hungry a crime, not just a tragedy!

What we need is the kind of program used for seat belts: blanket education through the media until seat belts were a given, not a choice. Distribution and storage are not a problem in the U.S. as it is in some developing countries. We have refrigeration, drying machines, farmers markets, food delivery services and other ways to meet the needs of the hungry.

So my priority would be to end hunger in the U.S. by eliminating waste, growing and manufacturing whole foods, and distributing it fairly to those in need. For one more person to succumb to malnutrition or a life-threatening disease because his or her body's immune system is weakened by lack of nutrients from fresh and lightly prepared whole foods is not acceptable in the country where I live!

ELLENSUE SPICER-JACOBSON
graduated from Douglas College with a degree in nutrition education.

For the past 35 years she has worked as a freelance writer
and runs the Menupause.info website.
She is the author of
The Whole Foods Experience: Everybody's guide to better eating.

RENEW OUR INFRASTRUCTURE

"This could provide some answers to those who are looking for work."

If I were in charge, the one thing I would do for the country is address the repair and renewal of the infrastructure. This would include the roads, bridges and tunnels that have fallen into disrepair, the electrical power distribution system (including the Ethernet that needs to be maintained in first rate condition all the time), water treatment and distribution, and, of course, the railroads. All these areas of concern have been neglected over the last 50 years.

The health, safety and welfare of all our citizens are dependent on a well functioning infrastructure. Not only do the citizens need a well functioning infrastructure, but the many companies that make and move product need this to prosper as well.

I would have Congress pass legislation that would provide funds for new and improved design of bridges, railroads, roads and tunnels etc. This would bring both the design and materials into the 21st Century. I foresee this undertaking lasting over 20 years as airports and railroad stations will need to be brought up to speed.

Such a massive project would provide many jobs in many fields: design, landscape design, construction, materials science, urban and rural planning, environmental science, technology, public art. This avenue of employment (similar to the WPA in the '30's) could provide some answers to those who are looking for work, needing to learn a new trade, and could even offer apprenticeships to many of the young men who are marking time in our overcrowded prisons.

If the infrastructure were in tip-top shape, I foresee the country functioning in a healthier way physically, economically, and socially. The well functioning infrastructure will offer opportunity to many who have been passed by in the current economy. It would give a boost to the general public who often don't see a direct benefit that will be so obvious to all.

CAROL SPONG

grew up in Massachusetts and now lives in San Diego. She currently works as an independent interior designer there. She is a wife, mother and grandmother who enjoys yoga, walking, reading and being with good friends.

ALTER THE TONE AND SUBSTANCE
OF OUR NATIONAL DIALOGUE

> *"Long-term support for free market policies depends upon our system delivering growth."*

If I could change one thing, I would change the tone of our national dialogue by…

- Affirming that tolerance and courtesy are our national standards for conduct between Americans.

- Affirming that choices about family planning are individual and family decisions.

- Affirming that there is currently too much "God" in politics and not enough ethics.

- Affirming that capitalism and representative democracy are together the best engine ever designed for raising standards of living. But that long-term support for free market policies depends upon our system delivering growth, securing the environment, supporting the aged and providing a bridge across the wealth gap for those willing to work for it.

- Affirming that taxes should be a means for funding the government and lowering inequality, not for explicitly punishing those who have been successful.

- Acknowledging that capitalists have been known to behave badly and companies and their executives must be subject to regulation, fines and criminal enforcement for behaviors involving pollution, price collusion and other crimes that can be proven.

- Paying our respects to the heroes of capitalism: the men and women who dream up the products that become success stories, who have the courage to start a business, the fidelity to pay their taxes, the ability to create jobs and the imagination to provide innovative goods and services to the rest of us.

JIM STEINBACK

With a background in engineering, Jim was the President and Owner of Mangecraft Electric which he built into a successful company before selling to Square D (a division of Schneider) in 2005. During his career Jim has advised numerous companies and served on their Boards including Sage Enterprises, Amalgamated Bank and NASDAQ listed Corcom. Jim is also currently a director of RDI Group, Nightengale-Conant, and is the President and Director of a foundation for emotionally disturbed children.

APPOINT A CONSERVATIVE TO
THE SUPREME COURT

"Freedom is never more than one generation away from extinction."

My number one concern is with the U.S. Constitution and the Supreme Court. Without Justice Antonin Scalia, the Court is divided 4-4, with Justice Kennedy, and sometimes Roberts, being swing votes, but seldom voting together. Sometimes, the Court's decisions infuriate liberals (e.g. Citizens United), and sometimes conservatives (e.g. Obamacare), but at least there has been balance up to now.

Republics are fragile as many of our greatest leaders have noted. Benjamin Franklin questioned whether the new republic would survive for long, and Ronald Reagan, two centuries later, believed that "Freedom is never more than one generation away from extinction." This is so because men seek power, often in excess, and then wish to dictate how others should live. This is a mortal threat to freedom, which once lost, is seldom recovered. In our republic, the greatest threat to that freedom is always the executive. Its power was intended to be curbed by Congress, and especially by the judiciary, but if Congress and the courts refuse to perform that function, freedom is imperiled.

Over the decades, beginning with the Wilson administration, the executive has gained more and more power, with Congress becoming less and less effective. The Supreme Court has also accumulated greater power, writing into law any number of things that are not part of the Constitution's original understanding. The virtual repeal of the free exercise clause of the First Amendment is a good example. Roe v. Wade is another, and Kelo is a third. There are many more.

Progressives are the authors of these changes, and want more, but there is a great danger in this, since the more power is unchecked, the greater is the danger to freedom. Accordingly, if another liberal/progressive is confirmed for the Court, and a president elected who wants to enhance executive power even more than Obama has done, there will be few, if any, restraints on that power. Congress still has the power of the purse, but even that has been compromised.

Clearly, no new justice will sit on the Court until 2017. If a Democrat wins the presidency, there will be five votes on a permanent basis for the progressive agenda, and about one-half of the country will be alienated from the Court for a generation or longer. If a conservative wins (and that may or may not include Trump, who is a total unknown), a conservative will replace a conservative, and the balance on the Court will be maintained. This will continue the generally high esteem in which the Court is held now. It is the action I believe would most benefit our country.

BILL STOREY

was born in N.H, raised in N.Y. and moved permanently to California in 1957 where he graduated from Santa Barbara High School in 1959, and from the University of California at Berkeley with a degree in political science. He was active in student affairs and had a CORO Foundation Internship in Public Affairs in San Francisco, 1964-65. He worked in Sacramento in the office of Governmental Affairs, and spent about 25 years working for the California Postsecondary Commission before retiring.

MAKE IMMIGRATION REFORM A PRIORITY

> *"Demand that those serving our Congress make immigration reform a priority."*

They are foreign wives and husbands, even parents, of American citizens; students whose visas have expired; refugees from political oppression; entrepreneurs wanting to start businesses; members of families already established here; illegals who have hovered under the radar for decades. So many different situations, so little attention paid to immigration reform. And yet, how does one reform a policy to suit such disparate situations?

If I were in charge, one thing I would do for this country—and the millions of people waiting in the wings or hiding on the streets—is demand that those serving our Congress make immigration reform a priority rather than something to be avoided at all costs.

Many wait decades for legal status and pay lawyers, often exorbitant amounts, to work through the overwhelming bureaucracy, even though they have attributes that would make them ideal citizens. But, of course, it's not an easy problem to solve. One reform will not fit all, but like health care and other issues, we must start somewhere.

<hr/>

SANDI STROMBERG
recently retired from MD Anderson Cancer Center where she was
a magazine feature writer and editor of the institution's high-
profile magazine and annual report. Before coming to Houston,
she lived for the better part of twenty years in Europe,
where she published more than 400 articles
in magazines and newspapers.

She is also a published poet and guest
editor of Mutabilis Press' fourth anthology,
Untameable City: Poems on the Nature of Houston,
released in December 2015.

CREATE A PUBLIC-PRIVATE PARTNERSHIP
TO FOCUS ON CLIMATE CHANGE

> *"I'd sponsor a top-priority public-private partnership tackling climate change's causes and effects."*

Climate change is the most serious challenge confronting humanity today and tomorrow. The overwhelming scientific consensus is that accelerating warming of the earth's atmosphere and seas is provoking a combination of climatic crises that threaten human settlements and survival. A partial list includes chronic drought and food shortages, super storms, imperiled fish stocks, and melting polar ice raising sea levels to flood worldwide coastlines.

Devastating damage is estimated to occur within 35 to 85 years. For example, scientists forecast that rising temperatures will make the Middle East and North Africa uninhabitable, creating a refugee exodus of historic proportions. The most recent U.S. Government analysis projects severe flooding of coastal metropolises. Swamped in tandem will be the entire Northeast megapolis from Washington DC to Boston, a corridor containing 50 million residents and producing 20% of American GDP.

If I were in charge, I'd sponsor a top-priority public-private partnership tackling climate change's causes and effects. The main source of the greenhouse-gas emissions chiefly responsible for global warming is the burning of coal, oil and natural gas for energy production and transportation. Blocking corrective action has been the fossil-fuel industry's cynical but effective funding of climate-change denial.

The first remedial step must be to drastically reduce those emissions through carbon pricing (either a direct tax or cap-and-trade). Complementary subsidies would promote technological substitutions, including solar and wind power for electricity generation and electrical power for motor vehicles and trains. Coal-capture-and-sequestration could be temporarily included in this strategy while coal-fired power plants were being phased out.

To reinforce curtailment of climate change's causes, we need measures to mitigate its irreversible negative effects. For America, the most catastrophic of these is coastal flooding. This campaign would combine erection of protective barriers with massive population relocations. The good news is that these infrastructure investments can boost stalled economic recovery and employ millions of workers, including those displaced by energy-industry restructuring. The bad news is that the campaign will require a dramatic expansion of governmental authority (and international cooperation) during a period when conservative, anti-government sentiment is paralyzing U.S. environmental leadership. Precedents also indicate that many coastal dwellers will refuse to move.

My reluctant conclusion is that the necessary national mobilization may not occur until one or more climatic catastrophes batter our country, taking thousands of lives and demolishing communications grids. That bleak scenario makes proactive leadership all the more imperative.

RUSSELL SUNSHINE
is a retired independent policy advisor to foreign governments and international organizations. His career spanning 40 years in over 40 countries included long-term assignments in India, East Africa, China, Laos, the Central Asian Republics and Sri Lanka. Russell's new memoir, *FAR & AWAY: True Tales from an International Life,* is available on amazon.com.

REPLACE THE FEDERAL INCOME TAX
WITH A NATIONAL SALES TAX

"Putting money in the pockets of Americans, especially the poor, is therefore my choice."

During the last eight to ten years the U.S. has developed highly challenging problems. Any publication would parrot off a huge Federal Deficit, income inequality, offshoring manufacturing jobs, declining race relations, rights for minorities and so on. It is truly overwhelming to pick one to solve as the highest priority. This being the case, the focus has to be on the most urgent, and the postponement of several urgent and important ones.

Putting money in the pockets of Americans, especially the poor, is therefore my choice. The proposed solution is to eliminate the Federal Income Tax and shift it to a Sales Tax, excluding food and medication. Total government revenue has to remain, as a minimum, the same. Obviously this approach will shift the tax burden to the wealthier tax payers and especially to the purchasers of luxury goods.

The fast enactment of this is daunting but doable since a wide spectrum of legislators, from pro Cruz to pro Sanders, should support it for their own reasons. While this is a single-issue subject, I cannot leave out the subject of EDUCATION. Education must be taken seriously again at all levels! The current entertainment versus education status quo will undoubtedly undermine the U.S. as a viable society and as an international economic competitor.

ANTONIO (TONY) SZABÓ

was born in Hungary. When he was 10 years old his family moved to Venezuela. He received a Chemical Engineering Degree from the University of Houston, then returned to Venezuela. Mr. Szabó is now a U.S. Citizen having spent the last 25 years in this country. Because of his Petroleum Industry background he spent a number of years studying political and geopolitical developments.

Mr. Szabó has been in leadership roles, driving strategy and growth in companies for more than twenty years including the position as CEO of Stone Bond Technologies, his current company. Mr. Szabó is married, has two sons, and feels a significant passion for classical music and his instrument, the violin.

RAISE TAXES FOR THE RICH AND WAGES FOR THE POOR

"This income gap is not good for the country."

I'm doing my doctoral work in education so that's the issue that I care most about, but if I answer this question in terms of what I believe will most benefit the country, the issue I choose is income distribution and the outsized concentration of wealth among such a small percent of Americans. This income gap is not good for the country. It skews the political process, creates resentments and undermines the American narrative.

First, I think we need to adjust the tax code to restrict loopholes that allow the highest earning to pay a smaller percentage of their income than average earners. Yes, I think people with the highest incomes do need to contribute more generously to the tax base so that we can afford domestic programs that, in the end, benefit us all. For example, helping lower-income young people to get good educations ultimately benefits all of us when they become more effective earners.

Second, I think we need to address the minimum wage so that everyone who works a full-time job can afford to live. When I read about two-income families that still need food stamps to feel their children, I think I am not living in a first world country. My parents immigrated here from Mexico for a better life, and yet I see children living here in such poverty that it boggles my mind.

SOPHIA TANNENHAUS
is completing a Ph.D. in education at the
University of California at Berkeley.
Currently, she teaches Spanish to tenth graders
and works on educational evaluation projects.

RATIFY THE EQUAL RIGHTS AMENDMENT

"Legal and judicial systems continue to use the male experience as the norm, and the result is that decisions are repeatedly made that negatively impact women."

Lady Liberty stands in New York Harbor as a symbol of our country's commitment to liberty and justice. However, if she were an actual woman living in the United States, she would find that her own rights to "liberty and justice" are not specifically guaranteed by the U. S Constitution. If I had one thing to accomplish, it would be ensuring the ratification of the Equal Rights Amendment. It is an outrage that almost 100 years after ratification of the 19th amendment, the ERA remains unratified.

After the 19th amendment was ratified in 1920, suffragist leaders introduced the ERA in 1923 as a logical next step in bringing "equal justice under law" to all citizens. It was passed by Congress in 1972 and sent to states for ratification. Thirty-five states ratified the amendment, three short of the 38 needed. Since then the ERA has been introduced into every Congress, along with proposals for passage. There it seems to remain perpetually stalled.

Many suggest that now, the ERA is superfluous. We have laws protecting the rights of women, and most laws discriminating explicitly against women were repealed. However, unless the bedrock principle that equality of rights cannot be denied or abridged on the basis of sex is explicitly stated in the Constitution, the political and judicial victories women have achieved over two centuries are susceptible to being eliminated or reversed at any time. There is no need to look far for solid examples. Note recent attempts by some members of Congress to weaken Title IX, opposition to the Violence Against Women Act, the Fair Pensions Act, and the Paycheck Fairness Act and those who voted to pay for

Viagra for servicemen but oppose funding for family planning and contraception. Proposals in state legislatures throughout the country are even more outrageous - especially in states that have yet to ratify the ERA.

Legal and judicial systems continue to use the male experience as the norm, and the result is that decisions are repeatedly made that negatively impact women. The ERA would provide a legal imperative for lawmakers and judges to include equitable consideration of female experiences as they deal with issues of Social Security, taxes, wages, pensions, domestic relations, insurance, violence, and more. The ERA needs to be ratified now.

ANN TURNBACH

is president of Ann Turnbach & Associates, a firm specializing in human resource consulting services. She spent 23 years as vice president of human resources for the Houston Chronicle while simultaneously serving as the director of diversity for Hearst Newspapers. She was awarded the John Blodger Diversity Award by the Human Resource Media Association in 2002 and named Best HR Executive by HR.com in 2005. She holds a bachelor's degree in education from Bloomsburg State College and a certification in human resource management from NYU.

CHANGE THE WAY POLITICAL
CAMPAIGNS ARE FUNDED

> *"The average congressman
> spends about four hours a day
> asking people for money."*

If I had to pick one thing it would be to remove the money factor from politics. We haven't gotten rid of corruption in the U.S. – we have legalized it. "Campaign fund contributions" are simply legalized corruption.

I picked this first, because without reform of the money issue none of the other issues can be rationally solved or debated. Health care, guns, tax reform, energy policy, infrastructure, global warming, environment, education and defense issues are all being debated and decided by people and corporations with economic interests that are seldom in line with the public good. Take a simple issue like pollution inspections for cars. It can be done with sensors at toll booths and a camera, but the auto repair lobby wants to see your car every year for an "inspection" so they can sell you a brake job and an air filter at the same time. Each individual person doesn't have enough skin in the game to lobby the legislature so the auto lobby wins by default. It's the same with all the other issues, big and small.

There is another issue as well that is directly related to money in politics. The average congressman spends about four hours a day asking people for money (NPR, This American Life). For an honest, conscientious person this is a disgusting obligation. I think the U.S. suffers from a lack of honest, conscientious leadership because the vast majority of those people are put off by the process. By making politics realistically and sincerely free of corruption we might eventually attract a better class of politician: people who can work honestly to solve our problems. We need to end legalized corruption.

LOU VEST

Military family from Texas. Grew up in Air Force bases in Texas, Japan, Florida. High School in Kerrville, Texas. College at the Naval Academy in Annapolis; graduated in 1971. Married in 1975 to Emilce del Carmen Ballestas whom I met in San Diego and who was from Cartagena, Colombia. We have two daughters. After five years in Navy, I joined the Merchant Marine. Worked on ocean tugs as mate then captain until 1986 when I was invited to join the ship pilots association in Houston. Worked as a pilot for 30 years bringing ships in and out of port. Now retired. My side occupation for many years has been photography. I have had two solo shows and participated in various exhibitions in Houston, and my photos are in offices, terminals and public buildings all over the world.

GIVE ALL WOMEN ACCESS TO SAFE, AFFORDABLE ABORTIONS

> *"I think women should have the right to choose."*

If I were in charge of the country, I would work to ensure we had a national policy to allow any woman to get a safe, affordable abortion anywhere in the U.S.

I think women should have the right to choose. There is enough shame and guilt already heaped on women. Having no access to terminate an unintended pregnancy only makes it worse. I believe that if men got pregnant, we would not be fighting over this issue.

LINDA WEBB

has a doctorate in health care management and has for the last 30
years coached leaders and their teams from healthcare,
oil and gas and other industries in the Houston area.

CHANGE GUN OWNERSHIP LAWS

> *"About 33,000 people die from gunshots in the U.S. every year, with massacres almost a routine occurrence."*

If I were in charge, one thing I would do for this country is to make insanity illegal and socially unacceptable.

I refer to the particular form of insanity that causes otherwise normal people to want to own or be in possession of guns whose only purpose is to kill other people, or sometimes themselves. The only exceptions I would make are for law-enforcement and military personnel in uniform and on duty, and for bona-fide hunters with guns designed for hunting. Automatic weapons and handguns with large magazines are not designed for hunting.

The men who wrote the U.S. Constitution, with the Second Amendment ratified in 1791, were very obviously thinking of single-shot rifles, muskets and pistols, and could not have conceived of the mass-murder weapons that are commonplace now in the USA. It is so painfully clear that their intention was that the well-ordered militia should be ready in the late 18th century to defend the fledgling country against hostile invaders. People in the civilized world look on with incredulity as, in what is a fundamentally different world from 1791, even the U.S. Supreme Court is able to sustain the farcical notion that citizens have an essentially unrestrained constitutional right to their guns, and the country's leaders are afraid to attempt to change this.

The consequence now is that about 33,000 people die from gunshots in the U.S. every year, with massacres almost a routine occurrence, and it is no consolation that, as one gun rights advocate says, the 150-plus children who are killed by guns every year represent only a "tiny percentage" of the total.

This is true insanity.

The ultimate cure would take a long time and necessitate a fundamental cultural shift, but why not? So many other attitudes that once seemed entrenched and permanent have changed in recent decades; political and cultural leadership with courage and commitment could do it. I believe the majority of people would actually welcome it.

PETER WILKES

I am a British-born naturalized U.S. citizen and have lived in the USA for about thirty years. Until I retired, I worked in the construction business, based in Houston. I grew up in England where owning a gun was, and still is, unthinkable for just about everyone, except genuine hunters. I love America, and it has been good to me, but I wish it could be rid of its gun craze.

A CALL FOR PRAYER

> *"Do unto others as you would have them do unto you!"*

Our country is facing major challenges such as terrorism, economy, problems with Iran and North Korea, racial divide, etc. My focus is completely different and the current presidential race has magnified my concern.

It appears that we have lost our moral compass in many ways including "Do unto others as you would have them do unto you"! Trying to make someone else look bad never makes you look better. My concern is for our children and grandchildren and the terrible example that supposedly grown-ups are setting with name calling and put downs.

If I were in charge, one thing I would do for our country is institute a call to prayer just for a few minutes each day. I would ask people to pray for revival in our land that hearts would be turned to God for guidance and blessing. I believe when we have a good relationship with our Creator, we can then have a good relationship with the created. Just think what would happen if we as a nation tried to live by the example of the 10 Commandments. No one can do it perfectly, but trying would go a long way in living a better life.

RAINI DELONG ALTIMORE WRIGHT
was born in Dallas, Texas but has lived in Houston since 1966 when she
came to attend University of Houston. Married to Eric Wright
and between them have six children and their spouses
or significant others and, most importantly,
six grandchildren!

President of CAN Advertising which is a promotional advertising
company she founded in 1988. Past Sustaining President of Houston
Junior Forum, Founding member of Bluebonnet Society / Bluebonnet
Ball in Bellville, Texas, Past teacher in Community Bible Study
and other Bible studies, Member of Second Baptist Church

NEUTRALITY FOR SUPREME COURT JUSTICES

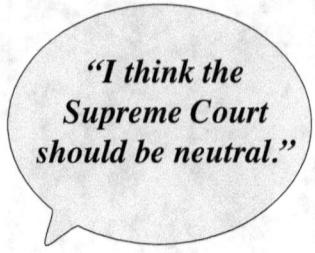

"I think the Supreme Court should be neutral."

If I ran the country, I would nominate a moderate as a Supreme Court Justice. I wouldn't use a "litmus test."

Previous presidents have nominated liberals or conservatives according to their own views with the object of creating a majority of justices to rule as the president and his/her party would, thus tilting the Supreme Court right or left depending on who is able to select the most justices. I think the Supreme Court should be neutral.

I would select a person who would view cases on its merits, not through the lens of ideology.

THELMA ZIRKELBACH
is a speech pathologist who works with young children.
She is also a multi-published author of memoir, personal essay, poetry
and romantic suspense. She is a mother and grandmother and also the
slave of a large orange tabby named Mango, who is smarter
than she is. She lives in Houston, Texas.

IV. VOICES OF THE NEXT GENERATION

*T*eacher Sofia Tannenhaus asked her tenth grade Spanish students at High Tech High in San Diego to answer the same IF I WERE IN CHARGE question she had answered.

High Tech High began in 2000 as a single charter high school launched by a coalition of San Diego business leaders and educators. It has evolved into an integrated network of schools spanning grades K-12, housing a comprehensive teacher certification program and a new, innovative Graduate School of Education. Its students are chosen in a blind selection by lottery without regard to zip code. Ninety-five percent of its graduates go on to college.

Here are 37 replies from Ms. Tannenhaus' tenth grade Spanish class students.

If I were in charge I would **make all public colleges tuition-free.** As low-skill jobs become a smaller and smaller portion of the job market due to advances in the field of robotics, it is more important than ever to make sure all of our citizens have access to a college education. If we limit college to only those can afford it we ultimately bottleneck our workforce and slow our progress as a nation. Another problem with our college system is that student loans are overbearing. Many graduates struggle to keep up with student loan payments as they move into the later stages to their life. We also see bright students decide that their family can't afford a higher education, which only slows progress and innovation.

Alex

IF I were in charge, one thing I would do for this country is **change the education system.** The current education system is based on a system that is more than 100 years old. With the introduction of the Internet, you don't necessarily need to go to school to learn anymore. The Internet is the most updated, comprehensive source for any information you would ever want. So then what's the point of attending a school now? The current education system is doomed for failure and, without change, students will keep losing interest in school and dropout rates will skyrocket. Education has many different values that only school can teach which can range anywhere from work ethic to making friends. Everyone has had at least one unforgettable learning experience from a teacher, whether that's positive or negative depends on the person. In conclusion, the world can become a better place if education is changed for the better. Right now schools are only barely beginning to take steps towards a new system. When that will be completed is entirely dependent on what the values are in the world. Is it war? No. Money? Maybe. Peace? Absolutely.

Fehung

IF I were president the first thing I would **change is the education system.** Our education system was established in the 19th century. This system is not effective in today's world. The U.S is ranked 14 out of 40 in its category. Children need a better education because, after all, they are the future of this country.

This education system is affected because of many variables such as poverty, student health, and much more. According to a 2016 Washington Post article, "Public Education's Biggest Problem Gets Worse," 22% of children in the U.S. are living in poverty and have a higher chance of dropping out of school, which shows how this system is not effective for everyone. If we want to make this country great again we have to start by solving this problem.

Israel

IF I were in charge, one thing I would do for this country is **improve immigration policies** and laws. As time has gone on this year, my class and I have really looked into immigration issues. Due to this, it has really made me realize how corrupt our system is with immigration especially from Mexico to the United States. If these laws were changed it would really make this country more peaceful as a whole. It takes way too long to get visas and to become a citizen.

These laws and regulations are causing hundreds of thousands to millions of people to go through great measures simply because they want a better life in the United States. These poor families are being separated due to their fathers and mothers getting deported while they are at school. If laws were passed to stop issues like this from occurring, our country would become a more peaceful place where everyone would be welcome to come and visit and or live.

This may seem like it would be a hard thing to have happen, but everything is possible with lots of time and dedication. I am very passionate about this, and if I were in charge of this I would find a way to make this happen quickly. My main goal in life is to make this country a more peaceful place to live.

Phillippe

IF I were in charge, I wouldn't focus on just one problem. I would spend time looking at each problem exclusively and individually, before using the resources of our great nation to solve them equally and fairly. I believe there is no problem greater than any other. To become a truly magnificent country, **our priority needs to be ensuring the equality and fairness of everything,** in every aspect of our lives. We must invest in ourselves. Many problems can correlate in the form of their solution. An example: one concern many people have is the gap between male and female wages. Another, separate concern is the gap between upper, middle and lower classes. In reality, these problems directly relate to each other, and can be solved with a single solution: A single class. By enforcing equal pay for everyone, regardless of gender, job position, and education, we can then truly be equal and fair.

If I were in charge, I would be the only person in charge. I would extirpate the current government, and restart from the ground up. As I formed a new government, I would create strict boundaries for our people that would help ensure an equal, single class. One of the greatest values to have, after all, is solidarity (synonymous with conformity). This is what I would do for our country, and this is how we would rise above the social norms to become the great nation we have the capability to become.

Garrett

THE problem that interests me the most is **pollution and how we treat the environment.** A pet peeve of mine is when people leave trash after lunch. I always feel like I have to pick up after my friends if they leave any trash behind. According to the Conserve-Energy-Future website, pollution kills more than one million seabirds and 100 million mammals every year. There are more than 500 million cars in the world and by 2030 the number will rise to one billion. This means pollution levels will increase by more than double. Approximately 14 billion pounds of trash, according to the same website, are dumped into the ocean each year, with a majority of that being plastic. Some problems arising from pollution can be too hard to solve or too expensive. We cannot stop automobile production, so the pollution coming from cars will continue to happen. Electric and hybrid cars are now being manufactured, which decrease the environmental impact, but these cars are not affordable for everyone. From a consumer perspective, the Prius is not aesthetically pleasing, which contributes to people not wanting to buy it. To solve the issue of pollution, one start is for markets to begin producing many more biodegradable products.

Matthew

 I believe one of the U.S's most prominent issues is poverty. Every day hundreds of thousands of homeless and impoverished Americans do not have a roof over their head or even food to eat. As well, these people are going through tremendous hardship; the amount of hate crimes against homeless Americans is appalling. According to The National Coalition for the Homeless, in 2010, there were 113 violent attacks against the homeless, with 24 of those resulting in death. Something as simple **as supporting state legislative efforts to add homeless persons as a protected class to state hate crime statutes, or advocating against city measures that criminalize homelessness** and for more constructive approaches to homelessness, could help improve the situation many homeless Americans are in today.

Autrina

 IF I could change something in this country I would **change the healthcare system.** Now I know you might be thinking, "why would you do this? Healthcare is important" Well even though it's a good idea and I would love it if it was truly possible to get a good working health care system in this

country, the reality is that it's negatively affecting our country more than helping our country according to a 2015 article by Fox news. (I know people will say that this is a biased news channel but so is every news channel). A report by the Congressional Budget Office estimates that

> The Affordable Care Act will make the labor supply shrink by 0.86 percent in 2025. This amounts to shrinkage equivalent to approximately 2 million full-time workers. The nonpartisan CBO estimates that the decline will come primarily due to workers responding to changes made by the law to federal programs and tax policy. The agency points to the introduction of health care subsidies tied to income as a key factor -- which in turn raises effective tax rates as someone's earnings rise, therefore reducing the amount of work Americans choose to do." Subsidies decline as income increases, reducing the return on earning additional income...that decline is effectively an increase in recipients' effective marginal tax rate, so it generally reduces their work incentives through the substitution effect.

To summarize, people will be losing their jobs over time. Now there are people that will be saying, "Oh what about Canada and their healthcare system, I mean, it's free" Well yes and no because healthcare is paid for through taxes. The quality of the health care in Canada is terrible; take a look at a video called, "Louder With Crowder," which is about the Canadian healthcare system. Also, if you look at other countries with a universal healthcare system, such as Greece, Italy, France, and Egypt, among others, their GDP is lower within the overall world standard.

I would change this by making this into a more of a capitalistic society. "Oh, but capitalism is bad isn't it?" Well this country was founded on capitalism and the U.S. is the most **SUCCESSFUL** country in the world because of the free market. Now if this change actually happened, you wouldn't have to pay for healthcare if you didn't want it.

Andrew

———◆◆◆———

IF I were in charge, one thing I would fix in America is **hunger.** One in six people in America are faced with hunger each day. That is too many people who have nothing to eat. The fact that there are people out there who don't know

when the next time they are going to eat is saddening for me. Forty-nine million Americans struggle to put food on the table, while there are millions of other people who have so much extra food that most of the food ends up going to waste. Some people do a good job to help others who need it by contributing to food banks and pantries, which more and more people are beginning to rely on. I think something we can do that would alleviate this situation is to require restaurants to give edible leftovers to impoverished and homeless people who cannot provide for themselves. When dining at a restaurant, you can clearly see how much food is thrown out. If there was a system in which food establishments were able to give uneaten food to someone less fortunate, it wouldn't completely solve the problem but it would benefit a lot more people.

Isabel

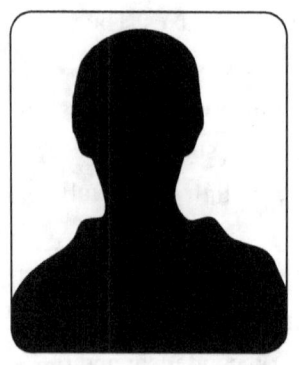

IF **everyone were free to be who they wanted it would make everyone happier** for who they were and people of all races and stories could follow their dreams. I think that it is a big problem in America and in the world that people are pushed to fit into society and work to be the top of some large company like Google or Nike. It prevents children and adults from following their dreams of being what they truly want. Did you ever want to be an astronaut so that you could explore space? Have you ever wanted to be an archaeologist so you can fulfill your dream of seeing real life dinosaurs? My dream is to be a pirate and sail the oceans as free as the wind, hunting for treasure and going on wild adventures. No one will ever tell me to go for it and become a pirate... instead, they just tell me to find new interests or find a new dream. I think that if I were the leader of this country, I would lead it to a completely libertarian place where you could do whatever you want and be whatever you want.

Griffin

IN my opinion, the biggest issue in the United States is peace and politics. It seems that the U.S. has many issues regarding terrorism. Politics are also a major problem. It seems that under-qualified people can run for president. Many are incapable to run a country and the idea and realism of that scares me. Many politicians feel that their values and methods are correct and ideal, that they are superior to other countries. The biggest problem with this is that none of it is true. The two-party political system has brought out the most extreme candidates. Rationality and qualification are not really required when they are allowed to run. I would like to **see a new system to make sure that candidates are qualified enough to run our country.** They should meet certain standards, beyond what is required now, and if they in any way pose a threat to our country's peace then they should not be allowed to run. Keeping peace is also a huge issue. With the way that the U.S. gets involved in other country's problems, playing a peacekeeper role, it causes us to have more enemies. Also, the threats made by some of the political candidates are heard by countries and people who are dangerous and can pose a threat to us. Again, this can be solved with a change in our politics as well as the U.S. taking a step back and maybe not being so involved. More thought should be going into the situations we put our country in.

Morgan

I think that one of our main issues is **poverty.** Our homeless population in San Diego is increasing and we are now fourth in the country. We have shelters to help with this issue, but there are not enough. If I were in charge, I would change this because we could have a better and more supportive community. What do I mean by this? People just need a little push, or some help, and if we were to help them, they could also become successful. Ultimately, these people could contribute back to society, as they would no longer need help from the government once they are working. Not having people living on our streets would also make our city look much cleaner. That's what I would do if I were in charge with a lot of other things.

Melany

IF I were in charge, the thing that I would change is **the way that our education works.** The United States is ranked 14th in education worldwide, which is not sufficient enough. Right now, many Asian and European countries are doing exceptionally well in education. If we put more money into education, it could potentially benefit our country more by having better schools, supplies and staff. I believe that more tax money should go into education instead of the military. I believe that if more money goes into education, the next generation will be more educated and be able to get better jobs. If Americans are highly educated we can create more jobs with higher pay. Another way that we improve education in this country is by making college tuition-free. This will allow, and encourage, more students to go to college. Many teenagers fear that college is too expensive and their families cannot afford it. If more tax dollars went into colleges, students would still have to meet the requirements to get into college but they would not be as worried about financing their education. These are the changes that I would like to see happen in the U.S.

Gabriel

I believe that **environmental issues are most important** at this point in time. Global warming, for example, has caused worldwide rise in sea level, deforestation, extinction of animals, and carbon dioxide and methane emissions. I think that by solving this issue it will solve other issues such as health and natural resource problems. If I were in charge, I require that industries worldwide, especially the ones that rely on fossil fuel, adhere to better environmental practices. Statistics from a 2005 study by a UN international monitoring group studied the increase of the human population in the past half-century and found out that the increase has already polluted and exploited more than two thirds of our ecological systems. We only have this one planet and we should take better care of it.

Isabelle

THE issue that especially interests me is peace and the environment in the United States. The human race is divided into so many pieces; sometimes it's difficult to find the good in things anymore. How can we hope for world peace when so many countries are constantly at war? Or when the people of a state are unhappy with how they're treated? It's disconcerting to know that it's going to be so hard to find peace for the United States. But it's the only way that we can save the world. Peace, saving the environment, it's all one big topic we need to figure out together as the people of the United States. Worldwide, people need to be aware of what types of environmental problems our planet is facing. Global warming isn't a theory, it isn't some dystopian idea someone made up. Global warming is a change that is believed to be permanently changing the earth's climate. We need to come together, find peace, and then work together to save our planet before it's too late.

We need to rid ourselves of 'single stories.' "If we listen to only a single story about a person or country, we risk a critical misunderstanding," warns novelist Chimamanda Adichie. They make us prejudiced and they darken our thoughts. We need to be compassionate of others' stories. We cannot be selfish, especially the leaders of the country. If I were in charge, I would **promote compassion, and create better standards to save the environment** of our country and help in saving our global environment.

Genevie

WHAT I would change in America is how corrupt our economy and our lives have become. We no longer see the importance of the problems we are facing but simply bring up a problem and then act as if we are finding a solution. During the past years, we have only gotten worse with the list becoming longer regarding issues like: global warming, bullying, poverty, politics, immigration, and war, among others. Instead, too many people are preoccupied with what celebrities are doing or what the next trend is. I think before we begin to bring ourselves to find a solution to one of the many problems, **we have to see if we care enough.** No longer seeing what is important, how can we surely find a solution to all these crucial problems if we don't actually believe in a significant solution? Sure we talk about bringing our world to peace yet don't bring it upon ourselves to do something about it. We mainly rely on other people who are relying on others and the chain continues. It is very disappointing how our reality has come to this. For a change in America, I would like to see this all happen one day.

Mayra

I believe that the biggest problem in the United States is our education. I believe that education itself is a big factor in determining an individual's future. Our society and the world, in general, need educated people to continue to function and to continue to advance in the future. It is important for children and young adults to be able to go to school, regardless of their financial status. The new generations of Americans are indeed the future of this country. Everything we have will be passed onto them, the most important thing being the knowledge we have. Many students are unable to go to college, and some drop out before graduating high school. We must improve the accessibility to education for young American citizens to better our country's future. We must also help encourage youth to continue to strive to learn and to finish school.

These people will all become a part of society, and we need them to be educated. To run a society, we need doctors, we need lawyers, we need teachers, and we need scientists, among many more professions that require college degrees. **We must try to help those who are unable to pay for school expenses. Money should never be the thing standing in the way of a child and a brighter future.** Education is the path to a better future for individuals, and overall is what brings mankind steps closer to developing a better world.

Annika

I think that one of the most important problems in the U.S. today is **systematic oppression affecting people's ability to succeed, especially those with unconventional gender identity.** Our society is designed for people in positions of power, and it always has been.

LGBT youths sometimes are kicked out of their abusive intolerant households, which contributes to their not graduating high school or going to college. Not continuing their education leads to homelessness due to things they can't even control and few career options to pursue. A law student at Williams Institute confirmed that 40% of homeless youth are LGBT. Many transwomen of color that need to pay for a medical transition, or even just food and a place to live, end up turning to sex work, which leads to untimely death; according to Planet Transgender, a transwoman is killed internationally every 29 hours. The grave fact is that the average life expectancy of a nonwhite transgender woman is 35 years old (Statistics provided by Planet Transgender). These young people feel as if there's no place for them in society, and there's no hope for them to become successful individuals, and we need to stop this so that these kids can see a bright future ahead.

Alec

IF I were in charge one thing I would do for this country is try my hardest to end child hunger. In 2014, there were 15.3 million American children who

lived in households with food insecurity. According to Feeding America, approximately 40% of all food in America goes uneaten each year, wasting $165 billion. There is so much food in America going to waste, yet numerous people are dealing with hunger. I would want to work towards ending this awful problem because no one should have to worry about when his or her next meal will come. The USDA estimated that $15 billion of fruits and vegetables is thrown out by supermarkets each year because they are deemed inedible, when most of the time they are still safe to consume. Even more food is wasted at restaurants where, according to Washington Post, about 17% of food is left uneaten. Overall, child hunger is a very big problem that needs to be solved.

Lydia

IF I were in charge, the one thing I would do for this country would be to **give NASA more money** out of America's budget. Currently, NASA gets half of a penny for every American dollar spent. In recent years, the once proud institution has had to cancel the space shuttle program and resort to only unmanned probes and piggybacking other nations' space programs in order to travel to the ISS. In the past, during the space race with the Soviet Union, NASA's Research and Development section was funded with more than triple the amount it currently has. A multitude of new domestic benefits came from this, with things like the invention of the common water filter, insulin pumps, and anti-corrosion coatings, among others. If we were to increase NASA's funding, would we not experience something akin to an invention renaissance? Simple imagination is all it takes to make America the nation that leads the world into space.

Zachary

ACCORDING to the National Alliance to End Homelessness, almost 565,000 Americans are homeless, many of who struggle with mental illness and are unable to receive the help they need. When I walk around my hometown of San Diego, I see many people in the streets who are suffering. America's wealth gap between middle-income and upper-income families is widest on record according to Richard Fry and Rakesh Kochhar. In 2013, the median wealth of the nation's upper-income families ($639,400) was nearly seven times the median wealth of middle-income families ($96,500), the widest wealth gap seen in 30 years when the Federal Reserve began collecting these data (Fry & Kochhar). I understand that we earn our money based on our work, but the U.S. provides foreign aid to other countries, takes in thousands of immigrants each year, and helps other countries as much as possible. Given the amount of spending on these things, we should be putting forth **more of an effort in helping our own people.**

Samantha

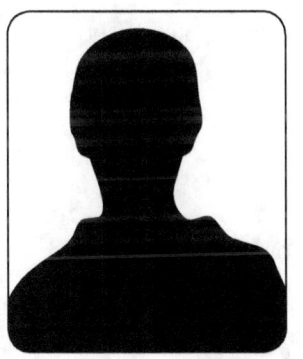

IF I were in charge, I **would direct the major stock and money holders towards a better future for the nation.** Our planet is suffering in many areas, both natural and unnatural. People only need so much money, and the top 1% holds 40% of the nation's wealth. I would not allow the top percentage of earners to be at that level of wealth and have the country they live in suffer. Do you really think a CEO works 380 times harder than his average earner? More than likely, those CEOs worked their way into their position. But does that mean they can sit back with millions of dollars that they can't humanly spend alone while Americans and immigrants suffer, right outside their door? Clearly money distribution is off center, and we need to wake up to the reality before the reality overtakes us and becomes unfixable.

"In the long run men inevitably become the victims of their wealth. They adapt their lives and habits to their money, not their money to their lives. It preoccupies their thoughts, creates artificial needs, and draws a curtain between them and the world." (Herbert Croly, U.S. political philosopher, 1869-1930)

Gabriel

IF I could change one thing in our country, I would **change the way people view capitalism and our government.** Both the ideology and the system are regarded as solidified, just structures whose means are not necessarily open to change. For years upon years we have self-righteously justified our actions behind capitalism without rightfully questioning the integrity or need for this specific system to be implemented in the world. Our country boasts the definitiveness of both while failing to acknowledge the crippling localized effects. With both major and minor issues becoming more apparent, it's clear that we as a country must be open to change and, in doing so, be willing to critique our flaws. In my opinion the first step to doing this is decreasing our stubbornness and ignorance about how to go about change.

Nick

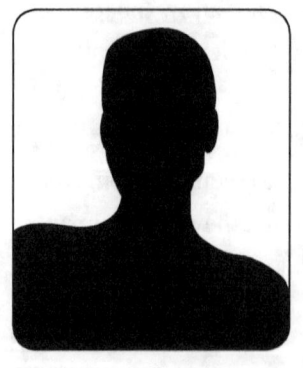

IT'S pretty hard to choose one issue, but if I had to it would most likely be something around **immigration.** Going into specifics, it has to be about people who have served in our country's military for many years who are not U.S citizens and have been deported for minor crimes such as marijuana usage or even something like carrying a firearm in some cases. Not only does it disrespect the war veteran, but it can also separate them from their families. If I were in charge, I would create a policy in which someone who has served in the U.S. military for at least 2 years would be granted American citizenship.

Garrett

There are many problems to choose from, but the one that I think is necessary is immigration. Immigration has caused many problems, like people going through hardship just to get a better life. It has resulted in many families splitting up due to mixed-status or the need to leave their home country to work in the U.S. in order to provide for their family. Many people go through so much hardship to cross into the United States. Parents in the U.S. that have migrated "illegally" will sometimes be caught by deportation services, leaving their children all alone. Placing children in foster homes after their parents have been deported can cause depression, among other struggles. Immigration has also caused a lot of tense family relationships. As seen in the documentary, "Which Way Home," children oftentimes grow up alone and angry in their home country, putting themselves in dangerous situations trying to reach their parents in the U.S. If I were to "fix" immigration, one way **would be not to deport parents of children under 18.**

Savreen

IF I were in charge, one thing I would do is **cut back on the amount of pollution we create.** I would do this by slowly cutting out traditional fuel-powered cars and replacing them with electric cars. The amount of cars that add to the layer of carbon dioxide is causing global warming by trapping heat from the sun in the atmosphere, which is causing the ice caps to melt. Normally, carbon dioxide that is created would be absorbed by trees and turned into oxygen, but with the rapid rates of deforestation, carbon dioxide has nowhere to go. Because of the effects of deforestation I would also have more trees planted and start the production of solar panels to be installed in uninhabited deserts.

Evan

IF I were in charge, I would **change the way women and men get paid for the doing the same exact job.** In 2014, women who worked full-time were paid just 79% of what men were paid, according to the Institution for Women Policy Research. Pay differences also depend on where you live; for example, the difference in pay was smallest in Washington, D.C., where women were paid 90% of what men were paid, and largest in Louisiana, where women were paid 65% of what men were paid. No matter where you live, women should not get paid a penny less than what any man makes, nor should they get paid more. In sports, men get paid more than women, but in the engineering field women get paid more than men because they want to motivate more women to join the engineering field. As a woman who is interested in bioengineering, I could get paid more than a man, which I believe is unjust. If I were in charge, I would make sure everyone was paid the same amount for the same work, no matter your gender!

Guadalupe

IF I were in charge I would change immigration. I would **make the process of obtaining citizenship a lot easier and quicker** by reducing the amount of paperwork, shortening the time it takes to get paperwork reviewed, and having fewer background checks. I would make the process no longer than six months. Normally it takes about a year or two. One way to make it more efficient is having more officers engaged in the citizenship application process. Funding would be a challenge, and it could come from user fees, government, and grants.

Elyse

MY number one issue is the **environment** because it is where we live, breathe, and eat. It is our home. It gives us food, water and shelter, all the necessaries we need to live. If we don't care for our planet, it causes natural disasters. Climate change, for example, has increased over the years, and global warming is causing a rise in sea levels, which leads to tsunamis and other disasters. If we do not begin to care for our planet, natural disasters will only happen more often and cause more death and destruction.

Nancy

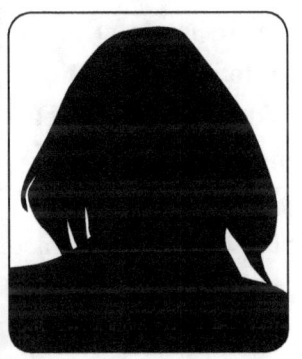

IF I were in charge, **men and women would receive equal pay for the equal amount of work** they have done. It is unjust that women work as hard as men, or maybe even more, but men still earn more in the end. If we are all created equal, then why can't we be paid the same? If I had a daughter, I would hate to tell her that she needs to work twice as hard because she won't be judged the same as a man. That is horrible to say, but sadly that's the world we live in. Toward the end of the recession, between 2009-2011, men gained 768,000 jobs and lowered their unemployment rate by 1.1 percentage points to 9.5%. Women, by contrast, lost 218,000 jobs during the same period, and their unemployment rate increased by 0.2 percentage points to 8.5%, according to a Pew Research Center analysis of Bureau of Labor Statistics data. Why do some women lose their job because of maternity leave? One in seven of the women surveyed had lost their job while on maternity leave; 40% said their jobs had changed by the time they returned, with half reporting a cut in hours or demotion

(PewSocialTrends.org). More than a tenth had been replaced in their jobs by the person who had covered their maternity leave. If children are our future, why are we bringing down the person that will raise them into someone important in life? You can call me a feminist all you want, but why do I have to be labeled when I'm simply supporting basic human rights? The solution would be simple: give equal pay to women and men for doing the same amount of work. This is such a basic concept that it is hard to believe this is a problem. Make life easier for both men and women, not just men.

Jennifer

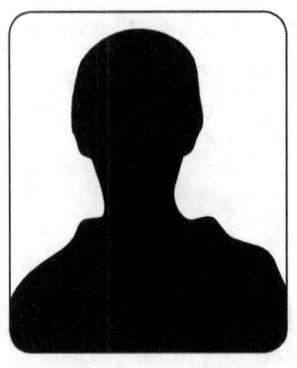

IF I were in charge, one thing I would do for this country is change the government system. Having a different president every four years causes a very inconsistent legal system and belief system. One president will make a new law and the next president gets rid of it, which makes things constantly change. Change can be good, but a nation with more consistency could prove to be more important. **A president should be president for as long as the majority of the people want him to be.** Whether the president should change, and when, should be for the people to decide. A maximum of 20 years could be set. This way Americans would worry less about who is going to be president next, and once you become used to having a new president, a new one would not necessarily be taking his/her place.

Connor

My dad regularly warns me about the dangers out there by telling me stories about unfortunate incidents he learns about. The point of these stories is to warn me to be careful, and his word has some truth. Some of his most common stories are about police officers using excessive force. Laws regulating police and federal enforcement have many loopholes. For one, in the state of California force is up to the cop's discretion and the situation he or she is in. Also, there is no law or rules for the use of excessive force. The basic levels of excessive force are verbal and physical restraint, followed by little force, and finally lethal force.

In 2014, a man and a woman were shot by Inglewood police officer, Lt. Scott Collins. Collins stated that he had stopped next to a car that was parked in the middle of the street and found the woman in the car had a gun. According to the police officers, the two suspects didn't respond when being asked to get out of the vehicle. The cops tried to "rouse them" even though they proved to be unconscious when they were shot.

Another story my dad told me about was a Carolina state trooper, Sean Groubert, who pulled over Levar Edward Jones for a seat belt violation. Officer Groubert shot him at least three times while Laver was attempting to get his driver's license and registration from his glove box, as he was ordered to do. Jones was lucky and survived the ordeal but with a hip injury that forces him to use a cane. Fortunately, he is expected to eventually make a full recovery. Officer Groubert was fired on the day of the shooting, September 25, 2014, and has charges pending against him.

There are more cases like this. Some police are starting to be required to wear hidden cameras to prevent these things from happening or to provide evidence. **I should not fear for my safety from our own police.**

Natalie

If I were in charge of the country, one thing I'd do is try to distribute the wealth in America. The wealth of the 400 richest individuals combined is more money than the bottom 60% of what earners take home (globalresearch.ca). According to the Thinkprogress website, the top 1% of Americans own 40% of the nation's wealth. I believe that this is a real issue because income tax takes more of a toll on lower and middle-class workers compared to those in the top 1%. The way I would accomplish this is by **creating higher income tax rates on the wealthy and putting that extra money towards public education and providing the poorest Americans with free healthcare**. Some might view increased tax rates for the wealthy as unfair, but the fact that CEOs can make up to 204 times the median pay rate of their company's employees is also unfair (glassdoor.com). I realize that the CEO of a company likely worked hard to get to where s/he is, but I don't believe that the CEO works 204 times harder than all of his average workers. I'm not saying America should convert to a form of communism, but I am saying that the wealth distribution in America is very skewed and needs to be confronted by our body of government.

Darian

 If I were in charge, I would put **more emphasis on the smaller third political parties.** More **specifically, the Libertarian Party.** Many people are unaware of this party, but it is so important because its principal objective is liberty. After all, America is called the "Land of the Free." Then why is libertarianism so neglected and given such little attention? Everybody in this nation is his/her own individual. People should have the right to believe what they want and do what they want (safely, to an extent) without this regime butting in and telling you how you may or may not live your life. According to lp.org: "We (libertarians) hold that all individuals have the right to exercise sole dominion over their own lives, and have the right to live in whatever manner they choose, so long as they do not forcibly interfere with the equal right of others to live in whatever manner they choose."

A Democrat or Republican can benefit from a libertarian government. But this party is so overlooked that people are completely unaware that a haven like this could exist. So instead, as of right now, we are at a loss in this presidential election.

Madison

According to the "Mapping Police Violence" website, 37% of unarmed people killed by police were black in 2015 despite black people comprising only 13% of the U.S. population. I find this statistic and many other statistics very shocking, upsetting, saddening, and honestly disturbing. If I were in charge, I would **ensure the complete safety and protection of this country's citizens with regard to law enforcement.** The reason this is so important is because if you're not able to manage a police force so that they lawfully protect and serve your citizens, then you will not be able to have an environment where those officers are accepted and trusted. Because of such a drastically high percentage of black/brown males and females being killed by officers, it would be in this country's best interest to reflect on why this is, but also hold those officers accountable for their actions. Unfortunately only 10 of the 102 cases in 2015 where police killed an unarmed black person resulted in those officers being charged with a crime. An important step towards fixing this issue is holding officers accountable by having them wear cameras. In the same way dashboard cameras have contributed towards solving lots of police cases, body cameras will be used to present evidence and will hold the officers accountable for their actions. By doing this, it will hopefully lower those staggering percentages, create a more comfortable environment for the country's citizens, and help enlighten law enforcement so that they can be more trusted in the line of service.

Noah

If I were in charge, I would **improve the education system.** Education builds our future, and therefore we should always seek to improve it, especially since we're in the country with the most opportunity and yet we are so low in the education rankings worldwide. Our schools are teaching students that the most important skills are memorization and test-taking skills, which certainly isn't applicable when you're an adult. We need to teach students to use logic in K-12 education. Once people attend higher-level schools (universities), we can start to teach more specific things that can prove useful for everyone's respective careers in the end.

Education should be the very first thing we strive to improve since it lays out the foundation for what the country will be like in the future. If our education is improved, then we will have our future become even smarter than our past generations and so forth, solving other major problems such as our nation's debt and lack of resources such as oil.

Ricardo

If I were in charge, one thing I would do for this country is **support people who are homeless.** Instead of letting them walk the streets alone and asking for money, I would help create more homeless shelters for them to sleep and live in. I would also hire people to help them find jobs. It would benefit them, and it would also make the streets a little less crowded and a little less dirty because from what I've heard and seen, people complain that homeless people dump too much trash around the places that they stay at. If people don't agree with what I would do, then I would tell them to imagine if they didn't have a place to stay or food to eat. It isn't fair. They might've put themselves in that situation due to poor decisions, but they deserve a chance to redeem themselves.

Bijan

*K*elly Williams teaches senior English at High Tech High. She offered extra credit to students if they chose to write a reply for this book.

Here are the replies from seniors in Kelly Williams' class.

If I were in charge, one thing I would do for this country is make our economy flourish. Nowadays, there is a lot of controversy concerning presidential candidates; however, the underlying apprehension is taxes and whether they will go up or down. One thing is for sure when our economy does well, citizens are happy. So when it comes to my personal decisions as the leader of this country, I would go in more of a new deal type of mindset. What this entails is the following: **encouraging private businesses to hire employees and improve their product/service with monetary rewards. Personally, I believe no one can do it better than businesses.**

Although I might be young, and young people usually tend to be more fiscally liberal, I have made up my mind by researching what works and doesn't work for improving the economy and creating new technologies. The government should not play a big role in making jobs or creating emerging markets. Our human capacity works best with intrinsic motivation and competition amongst others, not under heavy government restrictions.

Abraham

One thing I would do for this country is **direct more of our focus into STEM. Science, Technology, Engineering, and Mathematics are at the forefront of the modern world.**

Fewer and fewer students are pursuing careers in STEM. This is due to the lack of support it receives in primary education and the ignorance of how important it really is to everything in our world. As

we speak, the mighty United States is slipping from the top. It's as if our country is a fearsome eagle circling the sky in a downward motion, its time in the sky slowly ending. Many different factors have lead to this downward direction. I believe it is the responsibility of STEM educators to keep U.S. up in the sky. Today's engineers are innovative, adaptive, and have shaped our world in a better way. Tomorrow's engineers need to be ten times more innovative and even better with creative, out-of-the-box
thinking.

Our country and world face many unique challenges that very few thought might occur fifty years ago: machines have replaced many human workers in the industrial field; climate change is heating up the Earth; oil is running out, and a sustainable fuel is needed. Even with our progress in agriculture, people still starve. Tomorrow's scientists and engineers are the ones who need to solve these problems that the previous generation has left us. Our generation might not be able to solve them. The decline of interest and the archaic school system that hasn't changed despite the adapting world has really created roadblocks for our future generations. This is why if I were in charge, I would be the eagle and change our focus; instead of making things harder for our future, I'd make them easier and again soar high through the sky of STEM.

Drew

If I were in charge, one thing I would do for this country is fix the education system. The way our system works, students spend so much time in school yet hardly get any work done. The majority of the time they are at school, they are on their phones, playing a game, talking to their friends, or just doing anything else, wishing their life away to pass the time they know they are required to be on campus, waiting until dismissal time.

There is so much emphasis on attendance five days a week, seven hours a day, and it's simply unnecessary and frankly, a waste of time. As president, I

would require only minimal attendance for approximately two days a week.
This time would be a period for lectures and where students are able to get their questions answered. Then, for the remainder of the week, students would be able to finish their work online and not be required to sit in a class once they are already done.

Because the same amount of work would take significantly less time, students would be able to learn much faster. In such case, another thing I would do is incorporate the opportunity to work towards your associate degree in high school by having the opportunity for college level courses once a student's high school level work is exceptional. This way students go through the education system much faster and don't have to spend so many years of their life preparing for their career beforehand. They can get out into the world much quicker. This would make a better society.

Aleah

If I were in charge, one thing I would do in this country is **to make the educational system more accessible. The higher ed learning system we have today is very unfair for students financially.**

I am a senior in high school, and I am afraid of going to college because in the long run I know I am going to be in debt, which is something I really am not looking forward to. I understand there are student loans and financial aid opportunities but knowing I have to pay it back and that it continues to grow the longer I hold off on the payment is scary. This impacts my decision on what I will be doing for the rest of my life. I have a hard time trying to decide on whether to go to school and put my parents and me in debt or go to a community college and not get the full experience and all the other benefits of going to a four year school. If I were in charge, one thing I would change is the expensive educational system.

Branden

If I were in charge, one thing I would do for this country is **promote equality in every way. Every gender identity, sexuality, income, race, background, everything.** Every-gender bathrooms are something I would like to see, which are currently being spread across many countries. However, I want this to be even more widespread. Students at my high school have specifically brought up this issue, either because they are transgender, nonbinary (meaning they don't identify as male or female), or they just want equality for their peers. Having friends that are transgender and nonbinary, I know a little about how much of a struggle this is for them to deal with every time they simply have to use the restroom. (I'm not going to pretend I know exactly what everyone goes through because I never will).

Another example of this sort of equality is fitting rooms in stores. I have a friend who is a transgender male (female at birth), who greatly struggled because he would always be led to the female fitting rooms. When he finally was led to the correct fitting room by a store associate, this was a huge accomplishment for him. Something this simple should not be something he must put up with in his everyday life. **Having every-gender bathrooms, fitting rooms, and other things of that nature would help eliminate the discomfort many people feel as a result of being labeled as something they're not.**

I could go on about how high levels of education should be available to families of all incomes, about companies hiring based only on the applicant's skillset and not gender, about physical appearance, and much else. However, just know that if I were in charge, this is what I would do.

AnnaBella

If I were in charge, one thing I would do for this country is change our **gun laws.** Many people say guns are a problem in America, but I disagree. Many of the people who do obtain guns legally obey the laws and practice proper

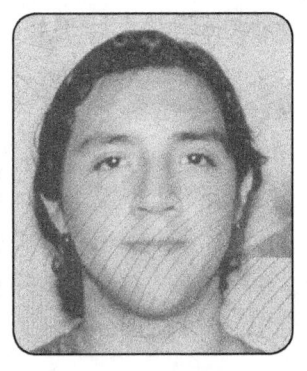

gun safety, myself included. And although there are many good people who do obey the laws, there are those who don't. Those who have committed crimes mostly get their guns illegally on the street, also known as the black market. There is also the gun show loophole where people can buy guns on site as long as you have the cash in hand, an ID, and a clean record, or at least say you do.

I think all booths at gun shows should require background checks just like at gun shop. But since people selling guns at the gun shows are titled as private sellers, they are not required to follow the same rules as gun shops. This is the case for many people at the gun shows, but there are a few who actually do run background checks, which is what everyone should be doing. This gun show loophole is why some criminals can get their hands on firearms. Another problem is people purchasing guns with mental illnesses, which can lead someone to go over the edge and shoot up a crowded place. This is why we should also focus. on the person's mental state before allowing that person to purchase a gun. These are the things I would change about our gun laws. This will empower those who obey the law and revoke the right to those who don't or who have a mental illness.

Ezio

If I were in charge, one thing I would do is change the way we farm animals. I believe **the way we currently farm animals on most commercial farms is cruel, and I wish animals were treated respectfully.** Up until seventh grade, I ate meat. I loved it just as much as anyone else. However, I stopped eating meat in seventh grade because of one school project.

We were assigned to study world problems and give presentations. Up until then, I didn't really think about where meat came from. I knew animals were killed for meat, but I didn't know how harsh and cramped the living conditions were on modern farms, or factory farms. I didn't know the animals were given growth hormones and all kinds of nasty chemicals. I didn't know their lives were sped up to be as short as possible just to increase meat production and that many are kept in cages in a large shed where most never see the sunlight. They spend their entire lives overweight because they can't even run around. Even fish and other sea animals actually also often come from farms, and if they are caught, the fishing industry is often as irresponsible as the farming industry. They don't care if their fishing gear harms other animals and if they are guilty of overfishing.

This one school project convinced me. I found it hard to stop eating meat because I enjoyed the taste, and it often is hard to find vegetarian food. However, my diet eventually became completely vegetarian because **I don't think it's right to eat meat when the animals are given such cruel lives.** I know that this country has enough empty land for old-fashioned animal farms, but they don't exist just because large companies prefer speed and money over the animal's wellbeing. If I were in charge, I would change this about the country.

Ethan

If I were in charge, one thing I would do for this country is **diminish the wage gap between men and women.** Women are often treated as second hand citizens when doing the same or sometimes even harder work than their male coworker. Why is it that for every dollar a man makes, women make 78 cents? How is this fair?

Let's say you have a man and a woman applying for the same job. Both have the same credentials from the same university. How do you justify compensating one more than the other? Research shows that 49% of the wage gap is because of the university you went to and what ethnicity you are. So what defines the other 41%? Because this has happened for decades, many women aren't aware of how big the wage gap is and how it continues to grow. Research shows that women often get paid less because they don't negotiate. Then, the women who do negotiate are often penalized for disobeying the social norm. How can we change the wage gap if women are guaranteed to earn less?

Morgen

If I were in charge of this country, **I would make every person learn how to play an instrument.** I strongly believe that musical proficiency would have a powerful impact on self-confidence, sympathy, and prosperity within the United States. Despite seeming trivial in comparison to homelessness, poverty, abusive relationships, and other notable topics, music fills a very important role in our everyday tasks. We use music to entertain U.S. on road trips, pump us up before sporting events, and make U.S. feel relaxed after a long day. Music has a powerful role in controlling our emotions. This is the central idea behind why I believe the country would see significant improvements if everyone played an instrument.

First of all, music provides an outlet for people to express their feelings in a safe and understandable way. If people are upset or angry, they can channel their anger through a powerful piano song instead of yelling at their friends or family. When happy or sad, they can use a flute or a trumpet to transform their emotions into a form that others can appreciate. By providing everyone with a way to beautifully express feelings, instruments will allow those listening to sympathize and understand the player's point of view. In addition, musical proficiency provides everyone an opportunity to succeed in society. Whether performing on the streets or in Carnegie Hall, each musician has the possibility of using musical skills to make a living and achieve fame. Whether or not we perform publicly, we have, for a lifetime, the ability to entertain ourselves and our friends and appreciate the joy of music.

If each person in the country could play an instrument, all of U.S. would develop individual skills and have a valuable talent of which to be proud. This would help people to gain self-confidence, as it would allow them to clearly see how their individual talents and musical interests make them valuable and important. Musical proficiency would allow peope to feel confident in their own abilities and understand their value to the world. It is clear to me that if we had a Musical Manifest for 'Merica, the world would be a better place.

Robby

⇒◆◆⇐

If I were in charge of this country, **I would reinvigorate the underlying inventiveness that once dominated American society.** Where have our inventors gone? We are a nation whose success hinges almost entirely on our ability to perceive, comprehend, react, and create. Technological advancement is so integral to the character of our nation, but why are we not encouraging more young people to participate? It seems that the younger generations feel a certain dissonance between themselves and the technology that is so much a part of their lives; they consume but they feel they cannot create.

For the past three years, I've been a core member of my school's robotics team. We are called "The Holy Cows", or Team 1538. This involvement has had an impact on me I know will follow me for the rest of my life. I have learned after countless sleepless nights spent working on a robot that, while technology can be difficult, the rewards outweigh all the struggles it took along the way. I can hardly begin to describe the sheer elation I felt when I watched Daisy Chupacabra, our 2016 dodge ballshooting robot I had been working on for over a month, slam dunk a ball in the final seconds at a competition in Phoenix. From competing and teaching fellow robotics enthusiasts in China, I have learned that technology is something over which borders have no control.

If I were in charge of this country, I would ensure that every high school student has at least some involvement with the STEM fields. Not the begrudged involvement found in American high school math classes, but the enthusiastic involvement that comes about when students are truly engaged with their work, when they can observe the products of their labor in action. This is the kind of involvement fostered by teachers who are just as thrilled about the outcome as they are the process. If I were in charge, I would create a more vital STEM program in our American schools. This, in my opinion, is the key to rediscovering our country's inventive spirit.

Rachel

V. IDEAS MATTER

Why This Project Is Important

In the middle of musing about responses, I read a *New York Times* op-ed piece. "Learning Lessons From Outrage" (3/21/16) by Charles Blow. Blow was writing about what he hoped we were learning from the primary upheaval in the Republican Party. "We must stay awake and engaged, informed and involved if we are to continue to move out of darkness and into light," he wrote. And he continued to say that we couldn't just be against something.

> It's about being for something: nobility, honor, character, righteousness, civility and togetherness. We have to decide who we are as a country, not as an opposition force but as a positive, proactive force, and use all the levers of power to which we have access to bring our vision of America into reality.

Yes! This project is my way of trying to be a positive and proactive force, of using an ability to inquire and organize to access people's visions of America without the ugliness of today's party politics.

"Do you really think you can make any difference?" a pragmatic professor asked. If we don't do this, it certainly won't make a difference. I know just asking the question stimulated all kinds of conversations far beyond my ears. Whether people chose to respond or not, many talked about what great discussions resulted when they asked the question of their families and friends. Here is a sample: "I was in Massachusetts to see my brother who is ill. My children were there and my grandson. We were on our way to the beach, eating lobsters and clams, and the entire meal we talked about this question. It was great conversation." Or, "I'm sorry I didn't have time at the end of the semester to write a reply, but we have been talking a lot about this in the dorm." Or, "My husband has been researching his answer for a month," a friend told me, "and he probably isn't going to finish but it sure had him thinking." These are great outcomes even if they didn't yield a page in this book.

I know that doing this has expanded my understanding of where people are, what they care about and why. I have always written books I needed to read. I needed to read this book. I needed to have these conversations because I felt cynicism and despair on the move within me, and I know that cynicism is a lazy person's response. It deprecates difficult situations without contributing in any way to a solution.

Most of the people in this book do not have a direct ability to enact public policy beyond the opportunity to vote and, perhaps, to protest or advocate. I hope hearing voices of desire and reason will create optimism for the democratic process.

The Source of Our Ideas

> *There are known knowns. These are things we know that we know. There are known unknowns. That is to say, there are things that we know we don't know. But there are also unknown unknowns. There are things we don't know we don't know.* Donald Rumsfeld

It is natural to draw our ideas from what we know. The woman who has been nourished for decades by gardening wants to talk about nature education. The mother whose son is in prison has an interest in prison reform. An affluent retired executive thinks about taxes while his younger neighbor is drawn to education reform.

Seeing how personal so many of these Replies are – personal in the sense that they seem to grow out of our own experiences – I am left wondering if our elected officials don't behave in similar ways. Balletopedia.com tells us that in 2013, for the first time, the majority of men and women in Congress were millionaires. All are not rich, but all are earning $174,000 (not counting spousal or investment income) with health and retirement benefits. Given the costs of living in two cities, including a very expensive Washington D.C., many might not feel very rich. However, when the average U.S. household income is in the mid-fifties, our Congressional representatives are not poor. It is unlikely that eviction or food stamps or lack of medical care haunt these men and women. Can you care about these things if you don't experience them or, at the least, know people who experience them? Of course you can, as many of these answers attest, but don't our circumstances affect our policy priorities? Surely, having people of many different backgrounds and circumstances participate in conversations about policy on an equal footing leads us to wiser outcomes.

None of us, even those wearing hats labeled "expert," are smart enough to see all sides of things. Hearing the wide range of ideas people chose for this project underscores that. So how do we figure out "what we don't know we don't know?" It is harder than we think as described by writer Tony Schwartz in this review of David Brooks' book *The Social Animal* in the Harvard Business Review (7/26/11):

> Brooks' core argument is that the vast majority of us have very little understanding of why we make the choices we do, and that we're influenced instead by peer pressure; impulsive and reactive emotions; a deep and bottomless need for admiration and status; overconfidence in the present; excessive worry about the future; the evolutionary instinct to avoid pain and move towards pleasure; and precious little capacity to delay gratification. "The unconscious parts of the mind are most of the mind," Brooks writes. "[They have] a processing capacity 200,000 times greater than the conscious mind." Tragically, this interior domain remains largely terra incognita, a vast unexplored territory full of resources and potentials we haven't begun to tame or to tap.
>
> Instead of drawing on our rational faculties to more deeply understand our interior impulses and motivations, we too often use our prefrontal cortex to rationalize, justify, minimize and explain away the unconsciously driven actions we've already taken. "A man hears what he wants to hear," Paul Simon sings in The Boxer, "and disregards the rest."

So even the smartest of us can act in dumb ways. It's so easy. The best protection is to understand this and ask ourselves, all of the time: Is it possible I could be wrong about this? Is there something I am not understanding? I didn't start out this way, but I have ended up reading each Reply with this thought: What about this makes sense for me?

VI. FEDERAL BUDGET

These two pieces explaining from where federal revenues come and where they go are provided by the NATIONAL PRIORITES PROJECT. On their website, www.nationalpriorities.org, you will find the NPP mission:

National Priorities Project (NPP) makes our complex federal budget transparent and accessible so people can exercise their right and responsibility to oversee and influence how their tax dollars are spent.

The charts reprinted here can be found on the NPP website in color which may make it easier for you to read. Thank you, NPP, for permission to reproduce these two pieces.

FEDERAL SPENDING: WHERE DOES THE MONEY GO

In fiscal year 2015, the federal budget is $3.8 trillion. These trillions of dollars make up about 21 percent of the U.S. economy (as measured by Gross Domestic Product, or GDP). It's also about $12,000 for every woman, man and child in the United States.

So where does all that money go?

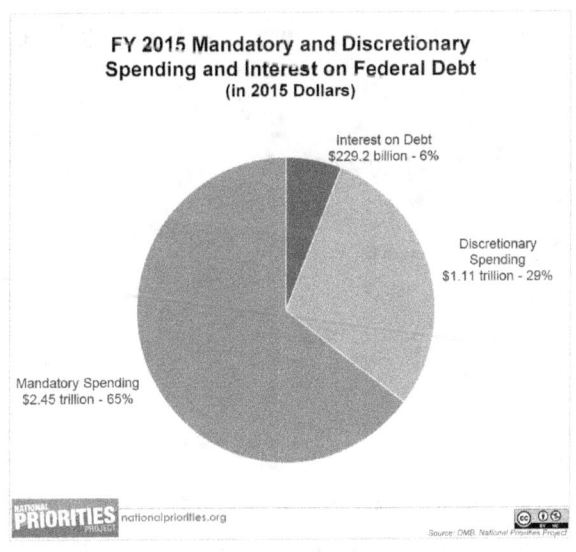

FY 2015 Mandatory and Discretionary
Spending and Interest on Federal Debt
(in 2015 Dollars)

Interest on Debt
$229.2 billion - 6%

Discretionary
Spending
$1.11 trillion - 29%

Mandatory Spending
$2.45 trillion - 65%

nationalpriorities.org

Source: OMB, National Priorities Project

Mandatory and Discretionary Spending

The U.S. Treasury divides all federal spending into three groups: mandatory spending, discretionary spending and interest on debt. Mandatory and discretionary spending account for more than ninety percent of all federal spending, and pay for all of the government services and programs on which we rely. Interest on debt, which is a much smaller amount than the other two categories, is the interest the government pays on its accumulated debt, minus interest income received by the government for assets it owns. The pie chart

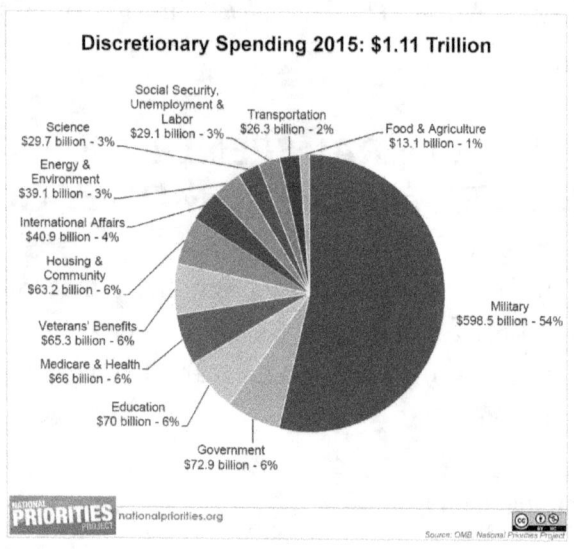

shows federal spending in 2015 broken into these three categories.

Discretionary Spending

Discretionary spending refers to the portion of the budget that is decided by Congress through the annual appropriations process each year. These spending levels are set each year by Congress.

This pie chart shows how Congress allocated $1.11 trillion in discretionary spending in fiscal year 2015.

By far, the biggest category of discretionary spending is spending on the Pentagon and related military programs. Examples of other well-known programs paid for by discretionary spending include the early childhood education program

Head Start (included in Housing & Community), Title I grants to disadvantaged schools and Pell grants for low-income college students (Education), food assistance for Women, Infants and Children (WIC), training and placement for unemployed people provided by Workforce Investment Boards (in Social Security, Unemployment and Labor), and scientific research through the National Institutes of Health (NIH) and National Science Foundation (NSF), among many others.

Mandatory Spending

Mandatory spending is spending that Congress legislates outside of the annual appropriations process, usually less than once a year. It is dominated by the well-known earned-benefit programs Social Security and Medicare. It also includes widely used safety net programs like the Supplemental Nutrition Assistance Program (SNAP, formerly food stamps), and a significant amount of federal spending on transportation, among other things.

Many mandatory programs' spending levels are determined by eligibility rules. For example, Congress decides to create a program like Social Security. It then sets criteria for determining who is eligible to receive benefits from the program, and benefit levels for people who are eligible. The amount of money spent on Social Security each year is then determined by how many people are eligible and apply for benefits.

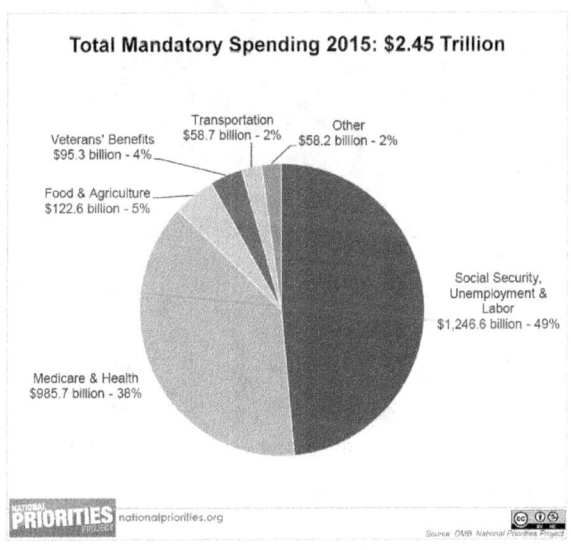

Total Mandatory Spending 2015: $2.45 Trillion

Transportation $58.7 billion - 2%
Other $58.2 billion - 2%
Veterans' Benefits $95.3 billion - 4%
Food & Agriculture $122.6 billion - 5%
Social Security, Unemployment & Labor $1,246.6 billion - 49%
Medicare & Health $985.7 billion - 38%

nationalpriorities.org

Source: OMB, National Priorities Project

Congress therefore does not decide each year to increase or decrease the budget for Social Security or other earned benefit programs. Instead, it periodically reviews the eligibility rules and may change them in order to exclude or include more people, or offer more or less generous benefits to those who are eligible, and therefore change the amount spent on the program.

This chart shows where the projected $2.45 trillion in mandatory spending will go in fiscal year 2015.

Mandatory spending makes up nearly two-thirds of the total federal budget. Social Security alone comprises more than a third of mandatory spending and around 23 percent of the total federal budget. Medicare makes up an additional 23 percent of mandatory spending and 15 percent of the total federal budget.

All Federal Spending

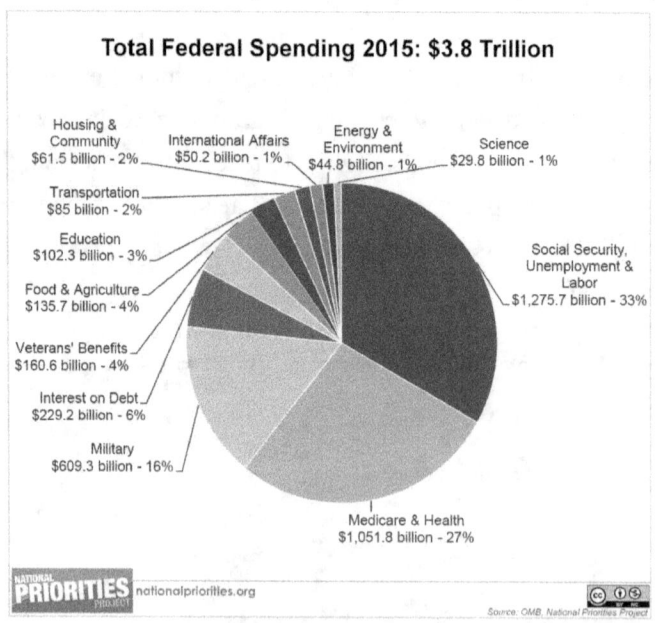

Finally, putting together discretionary spending, mandatory spending, and interest on the debt, you can see how the total federal budget is divided into different categories of spending. This pie chart shows the breakdown $3.8 trillion in combined discretionary, mandatory, and interest spending budgeted by Congress in fiscal year 2015.

Spending and Revenue

Here's how federal spending and revenue in 2015 add up:

Spending in the Tax Code

When the federal government spends money on mandatory and discretionary programs, the U.S. Treasury writes a check to pay the program costs. But there is another type of federal spending that operates a little differently. Lawmakers have written hundreds of tax breaks into the federal tax code - for instance, special low tax rates on capital gains, and a deduction for home mortgage interest - in order to promote certain activities they deem beneficial to society.

In fact, tax breaks function as a type of government spending, and they are officially called "tax expenditures" within the federal government. When the government issues a tax break, it chooses to give up tax revenue for a specific purpose - so both spending and tax breaks mean less money in the U.S. Treasury, and both reflect spending priorities laid out by Congress in varioU.S. pieces of legislation.

Tax breaks are expected to cost the federal government $1.22 trillion in 2015 - more than all discretionary spending in the same year.

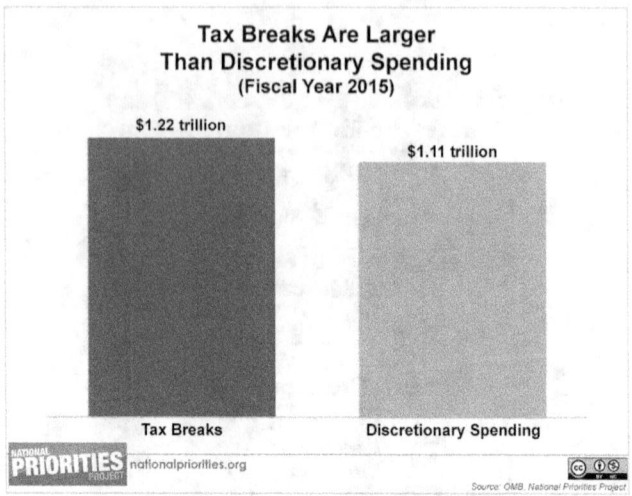

Unlike discretionary spending, which must be approved by lawmakers each year during the appropriations process, tax breaks do not require annual approval. Once written into the tax code, they remain on the books until lawmakers modify them. That means that even when tax breaks fall short of, or outlive their original purpose intended by Congress, they frequently stay on the books.

FEDERAL REVENUE:
WHERE DOES THE MONEY COME FROM

The federal government raises trillions of dollars in tax revenue each year, though a variety of taxes and fees. Some taxes fund specific government programs, while other taxes fund the government in general. When all taxes for a given year are insufficient to cover all of the government's expenses - which has been the case in 45 out of the last 50 years - the U.S. Treasury borrows money to make up the difference.

In 2015, total federal revenues in fiscal year 2015 are expected to be $3.18 trillion. These revenues come from three major sources:

1. **Income taxes paid by individuals:** $1.48 trillion, or 47% of all tax revenues
2. **Payroll taxes paid jointly by workers and employers:** $1.07 trillion, 34% of all tax revenues.
3. **Corporate income taxes paid by businesses:** $341.7 billion, or 11% of all tax revenues.

There are also a handful of other types of taxes, like customs duties and excise taxes that make up much smaller portions of federal revenue. Customs duties are taxes on imports, paid by the importer, while excise taxes are taxes levied on specific goods, like gasoline. This pie chart below shows how much each of these revenue sources is expected to bring in during fiscal year 2015.

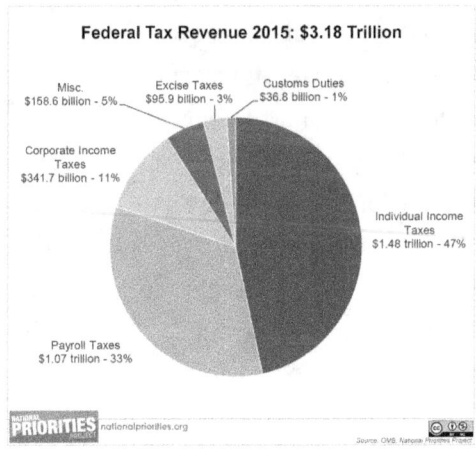

Federal Tax Revenue 2015: $3.18 Trillion

Once they are paid into the Treasury, income taxes and corporate taxes are designated as federal funds, while payroll taxes become trust funds. Federal funds are general revenues, meaning Congress and the president can decide to spend them on just about anything when they conduct the annual appropriations process (see our explanation of the federal budget process). Unlike federal funds, trust funds can be used only to pay for specific programs. The vast majority of trust fund revenues pay for Social Security and Medicare.

Income Taxes

The U.S. Constitution (Article I, Section 8) grants Congress the power to collect taxes. Early federal taxation was mostly in the form of excise taxes on goods such as alcohol and tobacco. Although an income tax existed briefly during the Civil War, it wasn't until 1913, with the ratification of the XVI Amendment to the Constitution, that income taxes became permanent. At that time fewer than 1 percent of people with the highest incomes paid income taxes.

Nowadays, more than 100 million American households file a federal tax return each year, and those income taxes make up the federal government's single largest revenue source. The income tax system is designed to be progressive. That is, the wealthy are meant to pay a larger percentage of their earnings than middle- or low-income earners. Due to the complexity of the tax code, however, this is not always the way it works out.

Corporate Taxes

Corporations pay income taxes similar to those paid by workers. Depending on how much profit a corporation makes, it pays a marginal tax rate anywhere from 15 to 35 percent. The top marginal tax rate for corporations, 35 percent, applies to taxable income over $18.3 million. As you can see in the line chart below, individual income taxes make up a much larger share of all federal tax revenues than corporate taxes do, in part because the wages and salaries of all Americans are much larger than profits of all U.S. corporations. The share of federal tax revenue paid by corporations has also declined substantially over time.

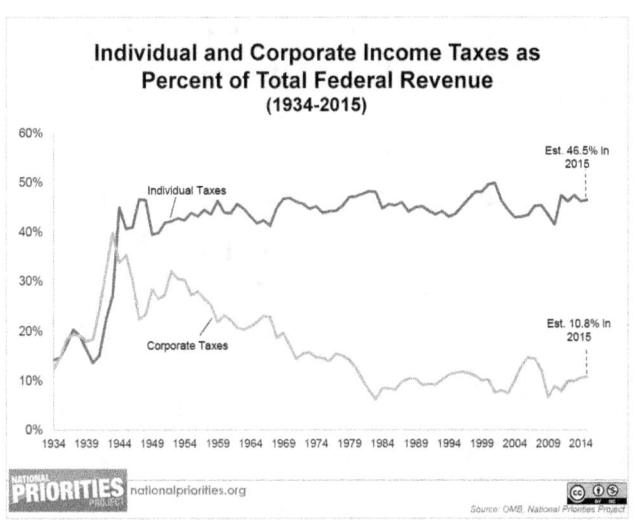

Individual and Corporate Income Taxes as Percent of Total Federal Revenue (1934-2015)

While the official tax rate for most corporations is 35 percent, the effective tax rate - that's the percentage of profits a corporation actually pays in taxes - varies enormously from one corporation to the next. That variation is the result of incredible complexity in the tax code as well as corporations' varying exploitation of "loopholes" to avoid tax liability. Loopholes refer to provisions in the tax code that exempt certain activities from regular taxation. For example, multinational corporations can allocate profits to overseas operations and reduce their tax liability by doing so. (For more about tax loopholes, see The Big Money in Tax Breaks.)

Payroll Taxes

While individual and corporate income taxes are designated as federal funds, as described above, payroll taxes are designated as trust funds. Trust funds can be used only for very specific purposes - mainly to pay for Social Security and Medicare. Social Security, officially called the Old Age, Survivors, and Disability Insurance program, is meant to ensure that elderly and disabled people do not live in poverty. Medicare is a federal program that provides health care coverage for senior citizens and the disabled.

Taxes to finance Social Security were established in 1935 as a payroll deduction - these are the payroll taxes you see taken directly out of your paycheck, labeled on pay stubs as Social Security and Medicare taxes or as "FICA," an abbreviation for the Federal Insurance Contributions Act. That's the law that mandates funding for Social Security by means of a payroll deduction.

The deductions from your paycheck are only half the story of payroll taxes. Employees and employers each pay 6.2 percent of wages into Social Security and 1.45 percent into Medicare. That means your employer deducts 7.65 percent of your wages from your paycheck to contribute to those programs, and then your employer contributes an equal amount, though you never see documentation of your employer's contribution.

Borrowing

In most years, the federal government spends more money than it takes in from tax revenues. To make up the difference, the Treasury borrows money by issuing bonds. Anyone can buy Treasury bonds, and, in effect, lend money to the Treasury by doing so. In fiscal year 2015, the federal government is expected to borrow $583 billion to make up the difference between $3.18 billion in revenues and $3.8 trillion in spending. Borrowing constitutes a major source of revenue for the federal government. Down the road, however, the Treasury must pay back the money it has borrowed, and pay interest as well. In 2015, the federal government will pay $229 billion in interest on the national debt. For more on this topic, see Federal Budget 101: Borrowing and the Federal Debt.

www.nationalpriorities.org

VII. ACKNOWLEDGEMENTS

This was a book was a collective community effort. I am so appreciative of all the help I received, not all of it acknowledged here. The smallest things matter when you are tacking your way forward with no blueprint.

I'm indebted to the people who responded and who trusted me with their ideas and their pictures. And extra thanks to those who passed on the request to play in the **IF I WERE IN CHARGE** challenge to others. I am appreciative of those who did not engage with the question but took the time to say why.

Thank you Sofia Tannenhaus and Kelly Williams for inviting your students to participate and organizing their responses. This was an unexpected gift.

I am grateful to Joan Son, Suzanne Kerr, Pat Cavenaugh and Lynn Rosas for early critiques and edits. Especially, thank you for valuing honesty first.

Thank you Jonathan Lieberman for tech support and advice on demand.

This is the third book on which Kelly Blakley has done the design work and she is a gracious and collaborative colleague.

The biggest thank you to my husband Michael who was so encouraging, nurturing and supportive for the entire obsessed five months of this project. If I could do one thing for the country, I would have more Mike Liebermans in it.

S usan Lieberman lives in Houston and San Diego with her husband Michael, a retired research physician who is a novelist and poet. She has a Ph.D. in public policy and a master's of city planning degree. She and Michael are the parents of two entrepreneurial sons and grandparents of five engaging children.

Susan has lived in seven cities. In Chapel Hill, she worked on a rural health project. In St. Louis, she was director of the Educational Confederation, an association of pre-collegiate independent schools. In Philadelphia, she worked on corporate philanthropy for the Conservation Company. In Houston, she managed community affairs for the City Controller before leading Leadership Rice, a program for undergraduates at Rice University. She has worked as an executive coach and a mentor for inner city high school students. Currently, she speaks to healthy adults about end of life issues and noodles over the question: How can we know when we are sure we are right but we are wrong?

Susan's books include:

New Traditions
The KIDFUN Activity Book (with Sharla Feldscher)
Venus In Blue Jeans (with Natalie Bartle)
Super Summers (Houston, TX, El Paso TX, Springfield Il, Jacksonville, FL)
The High School Handbook
The Mother-In-Law Manual
Getting Old Is A Full Time Job
Death, Dying & Dessert. Reflections on 20 Questions About Dying.

www.ingramcontent.com/pod-product-compliance
Lightning Source LLC
Chambersburg PA
CBHW071347280526
45787CB00001B/246